T0280054

LATINOS IN CHICAGO

LATINOS IN CHICAGO

Quest for a Political Voice

Wilfredo Cruz

Southern Illinois University Press
Carbondale

Southern Illinois University Press
www.siupress.com

25   24   23   22   4   3   2   1

Cover illustration: *top*, Harold Washington at a Campaign Stop, photo courtesy of
Carlos Hernandez, Puerto Rican Arts Alliance; *bottom*, Chicago Skyline from the
West Side with the Train, by jaflippo (Adobe Stock #210249480, photo cropped).

Library of Congress Cataloging-in-Publication Data
Names: Cruz, Wilfredo, 1954– author.
Title: Latinos in Chicago: quest for a political voice / Wilfredo Cruz.
Description: Carbondale: Southern Illinois University Press, [2022] | Includes
bibliographical references and index. | Summary: "Social history of the struggles,
frustrations, and eventual triumph of Latinos to achieve political power in
Chicago"— Provided by publisher.
Identifiers: LCCN 2021059882 (print) | LCCN 2021059883 (ebook) |
ISBN 9780809338832 (paperback) | ISBN 9780809338849 (ebook)
Subjects: LCSH: Hispanic Americans—Illinois—Chicago—Politics and government.
| Hispanic Americans—Illinois—Chicago—Social conditions. | Chicago (Ill.)—
Politics and government—1951–
Classification: LCC F548.9.S75 C785 2022 (print) | LCC F548.9.S75 (ebook) |
DDC 305.8680773/11—dc23/eng/20211220
LC record available at https://lccn.loc.gov/2021059882
LC ebook record available at https://lccn.loc.gov/2021059883

Printed on recycled paper

SĪU
Southern Illinois University System

For my wife, Irma,
and our children Alexandra Irma and Daniel Cesar.
A special dedication to my oldest son, Wilfredo Jr.,
keep up the fighting spirit.

And for my grandchildren,
Alejandro Robert and Mateo Jaime Cruz and
Christian Daniel English.
You guys are a bundle of love.

CONTENTS

Gallery of illustrations beginning on pages 55 and 103

ACKNOWLEDGMENTS

I wish to thank Columbia College Chicago for granting me a semester sabbatical. The time was most valuable in helping me to research and write a major portion of this book. I appreciate the work of Oscar Valdez, academic scheduling coordinator at Columbia College Chicago, for transcribing all the interviews. A thank you to Jacob Kaplan and Daniel Pogorzelski for helping to arrange some of the interviews.

Special gratitude is extended to all the individuals who allowed me to interview them for this book. I also extend a sincere thank you to the institutions that allowed me to use their photographs and archives. The staff and librarians of the following institutions were most helpful with research assistance: University of Illinois Chicago, Richard J. Daley Library; Harold Washington Library Center's Special Collections and Municipal Reference Library; Conrad Sulzer Regional Library; the Chicago History Museum; and the *Chicago Reporter*.

To my friends Eduardo Camacho and Ben Joravsky, thanks for all the inspirational political discussions we have had through the years over breakfast and lunch.

I am most grateful to Sylvia Frank Rodrigue, executive editor at Southern Illinois University Press; I appreciate your encouragement and assistance.

LATINOS IN CHICAGO

Introduction

The Latino community's first attempt to acquire a political voice in Chicago politics did not get off to a promising start. In 1911, William Emilio Rodríguez, a newcomer to politics, ran for mayor of Chicago as a Socialist. The mayoral race of 1911 seemed like a great opportunity for a member of the Socialist Party to sneak in and win the mayor's seat. Political writers Perry R. Duis and Glen E. Holt noted that "The major parties had been weakened by factional feuds, and reformer Charles Merriam, whom few gave much of a chance, had captured the Republican nomination. The Democrats ran former Mayor Carter Harrison II. Optimistic Socialists distributed thousands of handbills, and Rodríguez campaigned vigorously in all parts of the city."[1] But Rodríguez was trounced in the mayoral election and only managed to garner 24,825 votes, compared to Merriam, with 160,672 votes, and winner Harrison, with 177,977 votes.

Rodríguez was born in Naperville, Illinois, on September 15, 1879. His father, Emilio, an impoverished laborer, was a Spaniard, and his mother had been born in Germany and raised in rural Wisconsin. The family eventually left Naperville for Chicago, where William and his sisters attended public schools. Shortly after graduation from high school, Rodríguez joined the Socialist Party of America. William worked as a painter and decorator for fifteen years.[2] He graduated from John Marshall Law School in 1912 and worked in a small law firm based in the central business district of the city, the Loop. Rodríguez married Sophia V. Levitin and was the brother-in-law of radical journalist J. Louis Engdah, who was married to another Levitin sister.

Although Rodríguez lost badly in the mayoral contest, he was not a quitter. He firmly believed that as a Socialist he could use elected political office to help improve the lives of poor and working-class people. He had, perhaps, set his political sights too high by running for the mayor's seat; So, in 1914, at age thirty-two, he decided to run for alderman in what was then the Fifteenth

Ward (now the Thirty-First Ward) in the Northwest Side's West Town neighborhood. But again, Rodríguez was soundly defeated and only managed to get 2,177 votes against the popular Republican candidate, Albert Beilfus, who won with more than twice that many. Then, Beilfus died suddenly and the persistent Rodríguez announced his candidacy in the replacement election.[3]

Chicago, at that time, elected two aldermen from each ward in alternate years for two-year terms. The regular party concentrated their efforts on the race for the full term. This allowed Rodríguez to win with a plurality in the replacement contest.[4] With his 1915 aldermanic win, Rodríguez was one of three Socialists in the 1916 City Council. A Socialist newsletter of 1914 noted that Rodríguez was active in the labor movement for the past fifteen years. The newsletter stressed that Rodríguez, "Comes from a working-class family and has always stood with the people in their struggle for better conditions. Clean, clear-headed, fearless, and aggressive. Corporations have no strings on Rodríguez."[5] Rodríguez could not count only on support from Latino voters, as there were only a few thousand Mexican families in the city.[6]

Rodríguez won an easy reelection in 1916 and was alderman from 1915 to 1918. He took on the unpopular role of being a reformer in Chicago politics. He pushed for a city manager model of governance to take municipal administration out of politics. He spoke out against the city's transit companies, which, he charged, were making huge profits. He also became an advocate for immigrant Mexican families in the city. He criticized federal officials for conducting illegal raids in search of undocumented workers.[7]

Eventually, the voters, the two major political parties, and the press, turned against Rodríguez mainly due to his reform, his Socialist ideas, and his pacifism. He was against the United States' entry into War World I. During the war, a wave of anti-Socialist sentiment swept the country and Rodríguez's pacifism was widely viewed as un-American.[8] In 1918, Democrats and Republicans of the Fifteenth Ward joined their forces together to support a candidate against Rodríguez. Rodríguez lost the election by 266 votes. Rodríguez then ran unsuccessfully for a judgeship in 1933. He devoted himself to the practice of law until his late eighties. He helped to found the local division of the American Civil Liberties Union. He later moved to Phoenix, Arizona, where he passed away in 1970.

After Rodríguez's short reign as alderman, it would be a long sixty-two years before another Latino again sat on the Chicago City Council.[9] Why did it take so long for Latinos in Chicago to achieve a political voice in the "City

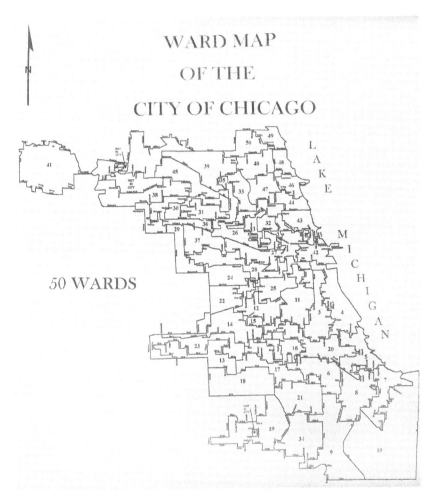

WARD MAP

OF THE

CITY OF CHICAGO

50 WARDS

I.1. Ward map of the City of Chicago. (Courtesy of Board of Elections, City of Chicago.)

of Big Shoulders"? That is one of the major questions this book attempts to answer. While the population of Latinos, mainly Mexicans and Puerto Ricans, grew significantly over the following decades, their political representation severely lagged.

Latinos wrestled with the problem of how to translate their population gains into some kind of political muscle. The Latino population grew steadily through the decades of the 1960s, '70s, and '80s. In 1960, the United States Census Bureau estimated there were 110,000 Latinos in Chicago, accounting for 3 percent of the city's population. By 1970, Latinos had increased to 247,343, or 7 percent of the city's population. And at the beginning of 1980, the census counted 422,061 Latinos, or 14 percent of the city's population, which then totaled three million. That was double their proportion of 7 percent in 1970.[10] Despite their population growth, Latinos lacked political representation; they had no Latino aldermen in the City Council, no ward committeemen, no state legislators, no citywide elected officials, few city employees, and no United States congressmen. All they had for many years was one Cook County Commissioner, Irene Hernandez; University of Illinois Trustee, Arturo Velázquez Jr.; and Cook County Circuit Court judges David Cerda and Jose Vazquez.

By 1980, Juan Andrade Jr., the executive director of an Ohio-based Latino empowerment organization called the Midwest Voter Registration and Education Project (MVREP), could name no place where the problem of Latino political underrepresentation was as severe as Chicago.[11] Over the years, the MVREP worked hard to register more Latino voters in Chicago and the Midwest. Meanwhile, Mexicans in various southwestern states were making great strides into electoral politics. Mexicans were being elected as school board members, city council members, state legislators, and even mayors. Similarly, Puerto Ricans in New York, New Jersey, and Pennsylvania were also winning political victories and being elected as city council members and state legislators. In 1970, Puerto Ricans in New York even managed to elect Herman Badillo as congressman from New York's South Bronx. Yet in Chicago, it was indeed baffling as to why Latinos found themselves outside the halls of power looking in.

Many excellent books have been written about Chicago politics. Yet interestingly, most of these books make little mention of Latinos or the contributions they have made to Chicago politics. It's almost as if Latinos were an invisible community for many years. This book attempts to fill in that void. This book is a descriptive social history of Latinos, mainly Mexicans and Puerto Ricans, and their long, hard struggle to achieve some political representation in Chicago. Of Chicago's 803,476 Latinos, Mexicans are by far the largest group accounting for 80 percent. Puerto Ricans are the second biggest group. There are other Latino groups in the city including Guatemalans, Salvadorans, Columbians, and Cubans. However, this book will concentrate mainly on describing how the city's two largest groups, Mexicans and Puerto Ricans were basically shut out of the political process for decades. They initially were not invited to sit at the table of political power. This lack of political power—or "clout," as it is known in Chicago—undoubtedly made their adjustment as

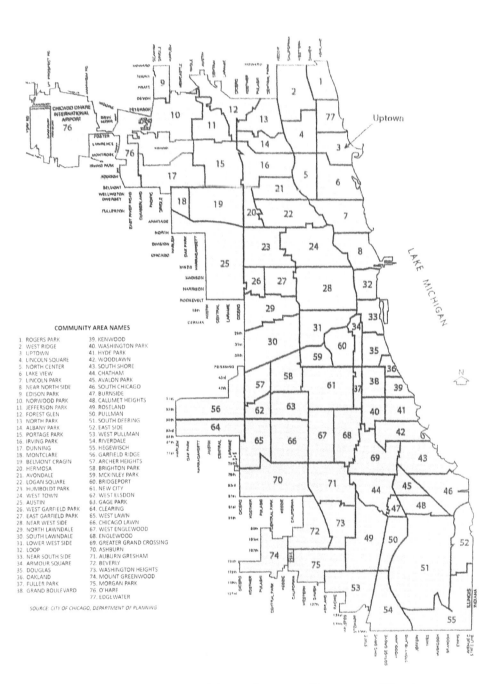

COMMUNITY AREA NAMES

1. ROGERS PARK
2. WEST RIDGE
3. UPTOWN
4. LINCOLN SQUARE
5. NORTH CENTER
6. LAKE VIEW
7. LINCOLN PARK
8. NEAR NORTH SIDE
9. EDISON PARK
10. NORWOOD PARK
11. JEFFERSON PARK
12. FOREST GLEN
13. NORTH PARK
14. ALBANY PARK
15. PORTAGE PARK
16. IRVING PARK
17. DUNNING
18. MONTCLARE
19. BELMONT CRAGIN
20. HERMOSA
21. AVONDALE
22. LOGAN SQUARE
23. HUMBOLDT PARK
24. WEST TOWN
25. AUSTIN
26. WEST GARFIELD PARK
27. EAST GARFIELD PARK
28. NEAR WEST SIDE
29. NORTH LAWNDALE
30. SOUTH LAWNDALE
31. LOWER WEST SIDE
32. LOOP
33. NEAR SOUTH SIDE
34. ARMOUR SQUARE
35. DOUGLAS
36. OAKLAND
37. FULLER PARK
38. GRAND BOULEVARD
39. KENWOOD
40. WASHINGTON PARK
41. HYDE PARK
42. WOODLAWN
43. SOUTH SHORE
44. CHATHAM
45. AVALON PARK
46. SOUTH CHICAGO
47. BURNSIDE
48. CALUMET HEIGHTS
49. ROSELAND
50. PULLMAN
51. SOUTH DEERING
52. EAST SIDE
53. WEST PULLMAN
54. RIVERDALE
55. HEGEWISCH
56. GARFIELD RIDGE
57. ARCHER HEIGHTS
58. BRIGHTON PARK
59. MCKINLEY PARK
60. BRIDGEPORT
61. NEW CITY
62. WEST ELSDON
63. GAGE PARK
64. CLEARING
65. WEST LAWN
66. CHICAGO LAWN
67. WEST ENGLEWOOD
68. ENGLEWOOD
69. GREATER GRAND CROSSING
70. ASHBURN
71. AUBURN GRESHAM
72. BEVERLY
73. WASHINGTON HEIGHTS
74. MOUNT GREENWOOD
75. MORGAN PARK
76. O'HARE
77. EDGEWATER

SOURCE: CITY OF CHICAGO, DEPARTMENT OF PLANNING

I.2 Community Areas of the City of Chicago. (Courtesy of Department of Planning, City of Chicago.)

immigrants to the strange, new city of Chicago more difficult. Their neighborhoods received inferior city services. In fact, for many years, Latinos had to engage in protests and demonstrations to get city officials to provide them with simple things like a street stop sign, a hot lunch program at the local elementary school, or regular garbage pickup.

This book will describe the various obstacles Latinos had to overcome, from the decades of the mid-1950s to the present, in their quest for a political voice. It examines how Latinos fared politically under the mayoral administrations of Richard J. Daley, Michael A. Bilandic, Jane M. Byrne, Harold Washington, Eugene Sawyer, and Richard M. Daley. The book looks at the experiences of Latinos who were eventually elected to political office in the past, and to a new generation of Latinos who are currently winning elected office. Finally, the book explores what the future holds politically for Latinos in Chicago. In terms of methodology, this book uses extensive interviews with Latino political figures and others and examines past court cases, newspapers, magazines, periodicals, books, archival materials, and historical documents. The book also uses photographs of many important political figures.

It took Latinos a long time to finally get a slice of the political pie. However, they now steadily continue to make significant political progress in Chicago, and their population in the city continues to grow. In fact, Latinos have now surpassed African Americans as Chicago's second largest ethnic group. According to the census: Latinos formed 29.7 percent of Chicago's population in 2016, their population climbed 17,751 over the previous year to 803,476. Meanwhile, the African American population dropped by more than 40,000 in one year. There were 793,852 African American Chicagoans, about 29.3 percent of the population. There were an estimated 882,354 White Chicagoans, about 32.6 percent of the population. And the census of 2020 showed the city's African American population continued to fall by nearly 10 percent over the past decade, with a loss of almost 85,000 residents. African Americans now make up just under 29 percent of Chicago, down from more that 32 percent a decade ago. Meanwhile, the Latino population grew by more than 40,000, and they now represent nearly 30 percent of the city's residents. White people make up 31.2 percent of Chicago's population. Today, Latinos are a rapidly maturing political power. Latino political empowerment is spreading in the city and the suburbs, and politicians and policy makers can no longer ignore them. Undoubtedly, Latinos will be key players in the political future of Chicago and Illinois.

CHAPTER ONE

Boss Richard J. Daley and Machine Politics

Early Mexican Immigrants and Deportation

Mexicans have historically flocked to Chicago in hopes of finding well-paying jobs and better economic opportunities. In 1910, there were only one thousand Mexicans in the Chicago metropolitan area. But over the following years, many more Mexicans came to work in the city's railroad, steel mill, meatpacking, and other heavy industries. The number of Mexicans working for Chicago railroad companies rose from 206 in 1916 to over 5,255 in 1926. Mexicans made up 40 percent of the total railroad maintenance crews of Chicago.[1] The first Mexican immigrants to Chicago were contracted workers. In subsequent years, many Mexicans came voluntarily to the city in search of work. Beyond Chicago, many Mexicans immigrated to other midwestern states to work in factories and heavy industries. By the late 1920s, midwestern Mexican communities emerged as permanent settlements with churches, small businesses, cultural centers, Spanish language newspapers, union halls, schools, and organized sports programs.[2]

Early Mexican immigrants in Chicago established mutual aid societies or *mutualistas*. In 1928, there were about twenty-three such societies in Chicago. Most mutualistas were small working-class organizations. Through monthly membership dues of a dollar or two, the groups raised money and provided food, clothing, shelter, and heating fuels to newly arrived immigrants and those who were sick or needy. Some mutualistas, or "sociedades mexicanas," as they were called, were formed by self-employed businessmen, who provided charitable duties and encouraged naturalization and voting.

Some of the early Mexican arrivals became naturalized US citizens. A few politicians reached out to these new American citizens, and they saw them as potential voters. A Latin American political club was organized in 1929 and hosted forums for candidates courting the Mexican vote in Indiana. However, the political aspirations of the Mexican population were stalled during the Great Depression in the 1930s and by the implementation by the Hoover administration of the Repatriation Program, which systematically deported thousands of Mexicans—many of them US citizens—back to Mexico during that same decade.[3] Nationally, almost 500,000 Mexicans, almost one-third of Mexicans in the United States, were deported between 1927 and 1937.[4] Unemployment combined with forced repatriation reduced Chicago's Mexican population from 20,000 in 1930, to 14,000 in 1933, and to 12,500 in 1934.[5] Consequently, the development of Mexicans in the Midwest was disrupted for at least a generation.[6]

Early Puerto Rican Migrants and Gentrification

Like earlier waves of European immigrants to the city, Puerto Ricans came to Chicago searching for employment opportunities. In 1917, the US Congress made Puerto Ricans American citizens. They came mainly as unskilled and often uneducated laborers. Their migration to the United States was dubbed the "airborne migration" as they arrived in airplanes. They migrated from Puerto Rico to the city mainly from 1946 to about 1960. In 1950, there were only 255 Puerto Ricans in Chicago. By 1960, there were 32,371 Puerto Ricans. Thirty years later, in 1990, Chicago's Puerto Rican population had more than tripled to 119,800.

Some of the first Puerto Rican workers in Chicago came as contract laborers. Castle, Barton and Associates, a private Chicago-based employment agency, set up an office in Puerto Rico to recruit men and women to work in Chicago homes and factories. In 1946, the agency brought 329 Puerto Rican women and 67 men to Chicago as contracted domestic and foundry workers. The employment agency offered a full year of work, and paid the workers' airplane costs, which they later deducted from their wages.[7] Some Puerto Ricans came as contracted farm workers to harvest crops in farms in New York, Florida, and California.

Puerto Ricans were also recruited as contracted laborers to work in heavy industries. In 1947, the United States Steel company brought several hundred Puerto Ricans to Lorain, Ohio for the National Tube Company, one of its subsidiaries. In 1948, the United States Steel Corporation brought in over 500 Puerto Ricans to work in its Gary, Indiana plant.[8] Hundreds of Puerto Ricans labored in the steel mills of South Chicago, Gary, and East Chicago, Indiana.

Puerto Ricans worked largely in unskilled occupations in the blast furnaces, where the work was unbearably hot and dangerous. Other Puerto Ricans came voluntarily to Chicago's Calumet area seeking work in the steel mills, meatpacking, and the hot foundries where metal was melted into various shapes.

Early Puerto Rican arrivals lacked educated professionals who could act as community leaders. Reverend Leo T. Mahon, an Irish Roman Catholic priest who spoke fluent Spanish, helped Puerto Ricans adjust to life in Chicago. Mahon was the director of the Cardinal's Committee for the Spanish-Speaking in the Archdiocese of Chicago. Reverend Mahon, along with neighborhood residents, founded the Puerto Rican community's first large organization, Los Caballeros de San Juan (Knights of St. John). The organization was founded in 1954 at Holy Cross Church at Sixty-Fifth and Maryland in Woodlawn. Backed by the Catholic Church, Los Caballeros established twelve affiliated councils throughout Chicago in churches with Puerto Rican parishioners.

Los Caballeros catered mainly to men and tried to keep them off the streets and instead focused on religion and family. The organization sponsored social activities like dances, pool rooms, picnics, baseball teams, and a fancy annual banquet in an elegant downtown hotel. They sponsored an annual El Dia de San Juan that included a small parade, banquet, and dance. The organization was not directly involved in politics, although Catholic priests did act as intermediaries when Puerto Ricans had complaints about City Hall. For example, priests complained to city officials about constant police brutality and mistreatment of Puerto Ricans by a largely Irish-controlled police department. In the early 1960s, Los Caballeros helped some Puerto Rican men prepare for, and pass, the test to become the first Latino Chicago police officers.[9] In 1960, the group organized Puerto Rican voters in support of the "Viva Kennedy Democratic" campaign.[10]

One factor that slowed the political progress of Puerto Ricans was gentrification. Since their early arrival to the city, they were displaced from the neighborhoods where they settled that developers subsequently found profitable and attractive. In the 1950s, Puerto Ricans were displaced from Lincoln Park. In the 1960s and '70s, they were displaced from West Town, Bucktown, and Wicker Park. Many Puerto Ricans could not afford the high rents, and million-dollar homes in these gentrified neighborhoods. Young, White, middle-class, urban professionals moved in.[11] The constant moving and resettling from one neighborhood to another prevented early Puerto Rican arrivals from establishing a stable community with solid organizations or a growing, mature leadership groomed for participation in electoral politics.

Today, some Puerto Rican leaders and politicians are attempting to stop gentrification in the Humboldt Park neighborhood, the heart of Chicago's Puerto Rican community. They created a public space that celebrates the Puerto Rican presence in the city. In 1995, these leaders and politicians encouraged the city of Chicago to build two fifty-nine-foot colorful steel Puerto Rican flags on Division Street. The area within the flags is a small commercial district known as Paseo Boricua.[12]

Mayor Richard J. Daley

Forced deportations and gentrification were obstacles that hindered and slowed the political progress of Latinos. The biggest obstacle, however, was the indifference shown toward these Latino communities by Mayor Richard J. Daley and his powerful Irish-controlled political machine. Daley did not create Chicago's political machine. Michael Cassius McDonald, a businessman who ran gambling operations and controlled patronage, created Chicago's first machine in 1871. Later, businessman and politician Roger C. Sullivan, and others, improved the machine tradition in 1894.[13] But it was Daley who perfected the art of running a formidable, well-oiled, urban machine. Machine politics revolved around power and control. They were organizations held together by a combination of ethnic identity and party loyalty. It was hierarchical and disciplined, often controlled by a single leader, a boss. They were built on loyalty and around an army of patronage precinct workers, ward committeemen, and city employees who delivered the votes necessary to get party candidates elected. The winning candidates controlled the government and distributed the spoils of patronage: jobs, promotions, city contracts, and city services as political favors to voters who voted for the party's slate of candidates.[14]

Mayor Daley and his Cook County Democratic Party simply did not try to help Latinos achieve any political power. In fact, Mayor Daley and his political machine were a roadblock to Latino political empowerment: they did not try to incorporate Latinos into the existing political system; they did not slate nor support Latino candidates for office; they did not hire Latinos for city jobs; and they did not offer city contracts to emerging Latino businesses.

On April 20, 1955, Richard J. Daley was sworn in as Chicago's fortieth mayor. He would be mayor from 1955 to 1976, a long twenty-one years. On the eve of his first mayoral term, Forty-Third Ward alderman Mathias "Paddy" Bauler, cheerfully shouted his famous words, "Chicago ain't ready for reform."[15] Bauler was right. While political machines were being replaced by reform-style government in many major US cities, Chicago had no intention of embracing reform. Daley preached that "good government is good politics."[16] However, Daley was not looking to be a good-government type. Instead, he ruled Chicago with an iron fist, like a boss and kingmaker. Daley had promised that if he was elected mayor, he would relinquish his role as chairman of the Cook County Democratic Party. But he refused; he insisted on being mayor and chairman of the Democratic Party. He consolidated his power and he used his immense power to reward friends and family and to punish his enemies. Machine politics amounted to "transactional politics," in which politicians helped their voters economically in exchange for their votes.[17]

Shortly after the 1955 mayoral election, William A. Lee, a union official, supporter, and lifelong friend of Daley, made the mistake of calling the mayor "Richard" in public. "Don't you ever call me 'Richard' in public," Daley replied angrily. "I am the mayor, and don't you ever forget it."[18] The mayor was known to have a temper and yell at his city employees at least once a day. Most Chicagoans called him "Da Mayor." Mayor Daley quickly moved to strip the City Council of their powers and show the fifty aldermen that he called the shots. Daley immediately reduced the City Council into a rubber-stamp body with very little power. Professor William J. Grimshaw stated, "When Mayor Richard J. Daley was elected in 1955, he stripped the city council of its budgetary authority, and virtually every other form of authority, and he ruled in a dictatorial fashion. His council floor leader, Thirty-First ward alderman Thomas Keane, regularly disposed of huge blocks of legislation in only a few minutes time. He plowed ahead after consulting with the mayor, of course, but without saying a word to his council colleagues."[19]

Latinos Ignored

Mayor Richard J. Daley basically ignored the Latino community for many years. Latinos were newcomers to big city politics and the mayor saw no need to reach out to them. Like most political machines in northern cities, Chicago's machine catered mainly to the Irish and other White ethnic groups. Daley wanted voters he could control and who were loyal to the party. New ethnic and racial groups, especially communities of color, were viewed as a threat to the monopoly on power held by the machine. Steven P. Erie, in his study of Irish American political machines from the mid-nineteenth century to the present in eight once heavily Irish cities including Chicago, stated, "Entrenched machines, in contrast, are selective mobilizers. Having defeated the other party's machine and rival factions, consolidated machines need only bring out their traditional supporters. There is little electoral incentive to mobilize newer ethnic arrivals."[20]

The growing Latino community was increasingly concentrated on the Northwest and Southwest sides. Mexicans were clustered in the Twenty-Fifth Ward in Pilsen and the Twenty-Second Ward, which included Little Village. Puerto Ricans were clustered in the Thirty-First Ward which included Humboldt Park and the Twenty-Sixth Ward which included West Town. One long-term problem in Mexican neighborhoods was that many residents were not registered to vote, and a lot were ineligible to vote because they were not US citizens. Some late nineteenth-century political machines in northern cities helped newly arrived European immigrants become American citizens in the hopes that would become loyal machine voters.[21] But Daley never reached out to assist Mexicans with naturalization or to help them or other Latinos with voter registration.

Amigos for Daley

Since Mayor Daley and White aldermen ignored Latinos, some Latinos decided to reach out to the mayor. In the early 1950s, business and civic leaders such as Frank Duran, Mario Dovalina, and Arturo Velásquez helped organize the Mexican American Democratic Organization (MADO). The first Latino political organization in Chicago, MADO acted as a liaison between the city's Mexican small business community and City Hall. According to Velásquez, "I felt there was a need. I thought that if we went to an alderman to get something done for us, they weren't going to pay attention to us because we had no power."[22] Velásquez was a migrant worker who came to Chicago in 1929. He achieved financial success with his jukebox company, Velásquez Automatic Music Company. MADO requested the mayor's help in obtaining business permits and licenses. The leaders of MADO believed it was important to build goodwill with the Daley machine to assist them in developing their small businesses and to ease their difficulties with local ward bosses.[23]

By the early 1960s, Daley appointed Colonel Jack Reilly, the mayor's director of special events, to attend to MADO's concerns. Mayor Daley did help some Mexican businesses get business permits and licenses. Daley viewed MADO as a loyal, nonthreatening, conservative business group that could help advance the mayor's political agenda. Eventually, MADO became part of the group known as "Amigos for Daley." Other small business groups also joined Amigos for Daley, including the Mexican American Chamber of Commerce, Azteca Lions Club, and the Illinois Federation of Mexican Americans. Throughout the 1960s, and up until the mayor's death in 1976, the Amigos group served as middlemen between City Hall and small Mexican businesses by helping them obtain permits, liquor licenses, and loans.[24]

Amigos for Daley held dinners, banquets, and other fundraising events for the mayor. They organized hundreds of volunteers to work in the mayor's campaigns. They made "Amigos for Daley" campaign buttons, signs, and hats. They consistently voted for the mayor during his five terms in office. But for all their efforts, loyalty, and votes for Mayor Daley, Amigos for Daley got very little in return. The mayor took the group and their Latino vote for granted. As loyal Democrats, most Latinos regularly voted for the mayor and White machine candidates in aldermanic races. In return, Latinos had hoped the mayor and aldermen would offer them some city contracts and some of the thousands of high-paying, city patronage jobs they controlled. To their disappointment, however, Latinos received few city perks or patronage jobs.

Under Daley, most of the city's patronage jobs were offered to his loyal Irish voters, his White ethnic voters, and, of course, to the mayor's family and neighbors. Many Bridgeport residents held supervisory city jobs with high salaries, good benefits, and guaranteed pensions. The Chicago machine controlled over forty thousand patronage jobs at City Hall and thousands more in other governmental bodies. "We had everything that wasn't police or fire or career civil service," recalls Daley's patronage chief Tom Donovan. "That gave us a lot of positions to put our people in."[25] Employees in most major city departments, including police, fire, and Streets and Sanitation were predominately Irish.

The machine gave some patronage jobs that were lower-paying and nonsupervisory to African American boss William Dawson, former Congressman, to keep African American voters controlled and willing to vote for the mayor.[26] By the early 1970s, however, African Americans became increasingly disillusioned with Mayor Daley's political machine. Black people filed lawsuits against the city's segregated school system and police and fire departments. According to William J. Grimshaw, "The city administration also fought all the way to the federal courts in an effort to maintain racially discriminatory personnel policies for its fire and police departments. After lengthy negotiations, these policies were also overturned by the courts."[27]

During the civil rights years of the 1960s, younger Chicano activists in Pilsen and Little Village viewed Amigos for Daley as very conservative. They saw the group as composed mainly of older businessmen—with narrow business interests—who were out of touch with the real needs of the Mexican community. Chicano activists did not interact with the group. Amigos for Daley finally won a small concession from Mayor Daley. In June 1974, the mayor appointed one of their members, Irene C. Hernandez, a longtime city employee and precinct captain, as a member of the Cook County Board of Commissioners. Irene C. Hernandez said, "I think he [Mayor Daley] did it because at the time we [Hispanics] didn't have anything. But all he had to do was say that he endorsed me and I got the nomination."[28] Some Latinos celebrated the appointment, others saw it as tokenism. Hernandez retired in 1994.

Mayor Daley gave a speech to Amigos for Daley at McCormick Place in March 1975, a month after his primary victory. He thanked them for their help in the election. The mayor said, "I am particularly pleased that the name of the sponsoring organization is Amigos for Daley—friends—and I assure you I consider you amigos."[29] "And," the mayor then told the cheering crowd, many of them wearing sombreros and "Viva Daley" signs, "there are many Spanish-speaking persons who work for the city government."[30] That statement was simply not true. In 1974, there were only three Latinos in the Daley administration: Miriam I. Cruz, who was Puerto Rican, the mayor's assistant for Latino affairs; John C. Sanchez, regional program director of the Board of Health; and Aurelio Garcia, commander of the Thirteenth district of the Chicago Police Department.[31] A 1974 *Chicago Reporter* study revealed that only 1.7 percent of the 40,876 full-time city employees, and only 1.2 percent of city officials, were Hispanic.[32] Amigos for Daley felt validated by the mayor's presence at McCormick Place. But the group's unquestioned loyalty for the mayor came with a heavy price, and undoubtedly hindered the political progress of Latinos. During his twenty-one years as mayor, Daley did not slate any Latinos for citywide political office nor did he help any Latinos get elected to the City Council.[33]

On the contrary, in 1971, some Latinos believed that Mayor Daley and his council floor leader, Thomas E. Keane, gerrymandered heavily Latino wards to deny them their supermajorities and make it easier for White longtime aldermen to get reelected. A group of individuals, including a Puerto Rican, challenged the ward map adopted by the City Council alleging that the ward boundaries had been drawn to avoid having any ward in which the majority would be Puerto Rican.[34] In the case, known as Cousins v. City Council of Chicago, the court found no evidence of purposeful discrimination. On retrial, the district court also found that the redrawing of the Thirty-First Ward (the ward in question), did not discriminate against Black people or Puerto Ricans. Some Puerto Ricans questioned the courts' findings. At the time, many Democratic judges were elected with the help of Chicago's political machine and owed their strict allegiance to Mayor Daley.

Fiesta Politics

Mayor Daley preferred to give Latinos "symbolic recognition" and minor services such as business licenses. He would fulfill his ceremonial duties to Latinos by attending their ethnic parades and being the master of ceremonies at the Mexican Independence Day Parade and the downtown Puerto Rican Day Parade. The young women crowned as queens from these two parades would be invited to City Hall to take nice photographs with the mayor. The mayor would don large Mexican sombreros and Puerto Rican pavas (traditional straw hats) at ethnic celebrations. The media loved when the mayor wore funny-looking ethnic hats, and the photographs were printed in the newspapers. When the mayor from San Juan, Puerto Rico, Felisa Rincón de Gautier, visited Chicago in the mid-1960s, Mayor Daley invited her to his office at City Hall where together they smiled, shook hands, and posed for photographs. The mayor would attend banquet dinners in Latino communities, press the flesh, and pose for photographs.

In the early 1960s, some Mexican mariachi bands helped celebrate Mayor Daley's birthday by serenading him and his family outside of their Bridgeport bungalow at 3536 South Lowe Avenue. Puerto Rican musical groups, playing traditional jíabro music, would also serenade the mayor and his family in front of their Bridgeport home to celebrate the Christmas holiday. Some Latinos felt honored that the mayor attended their ethnic parades and celebrations. Mayor Daley, who was a tough, experienced politician, probably viewed

Latinos as gullible and docile. Daley figured that all he had to do to please Latinos was to show up at their ethnic parades, put on their ethnic hats, and yell "Viva Mexico" and "Viva Puerto Rico." But a growing number of Latinos felt that Mayor Daley and White machine politicians were not interested in addressing the serious concerns in their neighborhoods and only paid superficial attention to them. Some Latinos believed politicians practiced "fiesta politics" in their neighborhoods by shutting them out of mainstream politics and showing up only for festivals and parades near election time.[35]

Thomas E. Keane

Another major obstacle Latinos faced was that powerful White longtime aldermen in heavily Latino wards acted as "ward bosses" and zealously protected their fiefdoms. They too refused to share patronage or power with Latinos. In fact, they stubbornly refused to even acknowledge the growing Latino presence in their wards. Thomas E. Keane was the longtime Thirty-First Ward alderman. The Keane family had controlled the Humboldt Park area's ward since the turn of the century and saw the ward as their "family business." Keane's maternal grandfather and an uncle had served as alderman. His father, Thomas P. Keane, served from 1931 until his death in 1945.[36] Thomas E. Keane took over the ward upon his father's death and became one of the city's most influential politicians.

Mayor Daley made Keane his council floor leader and he became the number two man in the city. Keane became chairman of the council's powerful finance committee. Keane practically wrote the rules of the City Council. Like many aldermen, Keane, an attorney, had real estate and insurance businesses on the side. He used his political influence and clout to make money for himself. Keane said, "Daley wanted power, and I wanted to make money, and we both succeeded."[37] Even though the ward had a sizable Puerto Rican presence, Keane's staff, workers, volunteers, and precinct captains were mostly White. "There wasn't even one Puerto Rican precinct captain."[38] Puerto Ricans complained in vain to the ward office and City Hall about poor city services. Their complaints went largely unanswered.

Joseph Berrios, former Cook County assessor, claimed that alderman Keane did help Latinos, although he was hard pressed to explain how. Berrios was one of three Latino assistant precinct captains in Keane's ward. "We got to meet the precinct captain and he had come to me, and I spoke Spanish. They were looking for some kids to join the organization and so I joined," said Berrios. "As a worker in the Fifth Precinct, we knocked on doors, talked to all the Hispanics, and made sure they came out to vote on election day. We encouraged them to vote straight Democratic ticket."[39]

Others, however, disagreed that Keane helped Latinos. "Latinos in the ward were taken for granted and they were a controlled vote," said Miguel del Valle, former Illinois state Senator and current president of the Chicago Board of Education. "My late mother-in-law lived in the Thirty-First Ward, and precinct captains would give her two bucks to vote on election day. One time they gave her a chicken. My father got parking tickets and he figured I can talk to the precinct captain so he could fix these tickets for me. Latinos would vote in return for favors sometimes."[40] Political machines in other cities also dispensed small favors and gave out good old-fashioned cash to voters on election day to persuade them to vote for their preferred candidates.[41]

Keane became Berrios's mentor. He fixed a speeding ticket for the young Berrios, encouraged him to attend college, and rewarded him with a full-time night job at the Chicago Park District to pay for college. After graduating from college, Keane helped Berrios land a city job as Chief of Parking Meter Collection. "I observed the people involved in the 31st Ward when it was controlled by alderman Thomas Keane. I just rejected what they were doing," said Miguel del Valle. "It was awful. There was no connection to the Latino community, except for a couple of individuals who were politically connected. They really acted like they didn't need us. They had their political organization."[42]

Eventually, Keane got caught up in corruption. He obtained insider information on 1,878 parcels of land available through a scavenger sale, which he purchased and then sold to other government agencies at enormous profits. In 1974, he was convicted by federal prosecutors of mail fraud and conspiracy. Mayor Daley looked sorrowful at the news that Keane had been sentenced to the maximum of five years. Daley said, "Keane is one of the outstanding municipal authorities in this country. And he's done a good job. . . . He will always be a friend, he and his family. I served with him in the [state] senate and saw him do wonderful things for the people of Illinois and the people of Chicago."[43]

Keane served twenty-two months of a five-year prison sentence. Keane was quite a character. Even from prison he arranged for his wife, Adeline, who had no aldermanic qualifications, to be slated to replace him as alderman in 1975. It was really Keane who ran the ward from his jail cell. Once, Adeline Keane was touring the ward and noticed a public elementary school. She said it was too bad they didn't teach Latin in the public schools. She didn't know that Latino children spoke Spanish and not Latin. "She blew it there," recalled Joseph Berrios, who worked for Adeline Keane and accompanied her on the tour.[44] Adeline Keane did not seek reelection in 1979.

Vito Marzullo

Second-generation Mexicans in Pilsen and Little Village complained during the 1960s and '70s that White, old-time aldermen loyal to the political machine represented Mexican wards. These White politicians, they argued, did little to improve their neighborhoods. Vito Marzullo was the Italian alderman of the Twenty-Fifth Ward, which includes Pilsen. He won office in 1953 and served more than thirty years as alderman. Like other White old-guard machine aldermen, Marzullo wanted to believe that the ward was still composed of White European immigrants, who needed him, his patronage jobs, and the small favors he dispensed. But White people had long ago moved to the suburbs.

In his mid-eighties, Marzullo spoke with a heavy accent and poor grammar. He had a knack for publicly insulting Mexicans with his racist rants. When asked by reporters, in the early 1980s, about the growing Mexican presence in his ward, he replied, "Sure, there are Mexicans in the ward. If you're counting the rats of the ward."[45] On another occasion, he said of Mexicans, "For God's sake, these people better learn something about America or go back to Mexico where they belong."[46] Ben Martinez, a Mexican precinct captain and secretary to Marzullo, also viewed Mexicans as a problem. Martinez said, "I'm seeing our ward and our precinct overrun with these people. It has a detrimental affect (sic) on our election results. They don't vote. They have no aspirations to become citizens. There's a state of apathy that exists in the Mexican community. . . . Why can't they get their papers, become citizens, and participate in politics?"[47]

Mexicans tried to put Marzullo out of office. In 1983, Juan Velázquez, a young community activist, ran against Marzullo but lost. Marzullo beat Velázquez capturing about 57 percent of the vote. In 1984, state representative Marco Domico also defeated Velázquez to succeed Marzullo as ward committeeman.[48] The contests underscored the inexperience and poor campaign organizing of Mexican candidates. Also, although Pilsen was about 65 percent Latino, many Mexicans were below voting age, and a large percentage were undocumented. Traditionally, Pilsen and Little Village had the lowest rates of registered voters in the city. In 1985, the eighty-eight-year-old Marzullo finally retired. Ben Martinez, with the Democratic Party's backing, became a representative in the Illinois General Assembly.

Community Activism and Protest

Lacking political power, younger Latinos in the 1960s and '70s voiced their concerns through activist community organizations. Pilsen exploded with manifestations of Mexican culture, nationalism, and political activism. Mexicans stressed "Brown Power," and began calling themselves Chicanos, attesting to their pride in Mexican culture and their new political consciousness. A new generation of community leaders emerged. Chicano pride was clearly evident in the large, colorful murals that began to adorn the walls of many buildings in Pilsen.[49]

Mexicans were angry that White politicians ignored them and their concerns. Residents increasingly got involved in demonstrations, protests, and confrontation politics. They took to the streets to protest against police brutality, insensitive immigration officials, dilapidated and overcrowded schools, and the inferior city services provided to their neighborhoods. In 1970, Mexican activists took over the Howell Neighborhood House in Pilsen, a former Presbyterian facility for Bohemian youth. They renamed the group Casa Aztlán after the mythical original home of the Aztecs. Casa Aztlán became an active cultural center for Chicano artists and painters. The group helped residents wanting to become permanent residents or US citizens. The group repeatedly held demonstrations at the Immigration and Naturalization office in downtown Chicago to protest their rude service and their arrests and deportations of undocumented workers.

In the early 1970s, Mexican women like Mary Gonzales and Teresa Fraga — astute activists and community organizers — assumed leadership roles in the Pilsen Neighborhood Community Council. They organized residents and used large demonstrations to force city officials to provide jobs, improve schools, and provide better sanitation services.[50] The group used protests and a student boycott to force the Chicago Board of Education to build the new, $8.9 million Benito Juárez High School in Pilsen in 1977. Benito Juárez was Mexico's twenty-sixth president and the first president of indigenous origin.

Young Puerto Ricans also voiced their concerns through street protests. In 1967, Puerto Ricans like Jose "Cha Cha" Jimenez formed the Young Lords

Organization (YLO) in the Lincoln Park neighborhood, which has a sizable Puerto Rican population. A former street gang, the YLO was similar to the Black Panthers. In 1969, the YLO occupied the administration building of McCormick Theological Seminary. They wanted the seminary and the city to help poor people on the Near North Side.[51] Later that year, the YLO took over the Armitage United Methodist Church where they opened a day care center and breakfast program in the church's basement. The YLO opposed the city's plans to revitalize and gentrify Lincoln Park because they feared the Puerto Rican community would be displaced. On January 23, 1969, the Young Lords barged into a meeting of the Lincoln Park Community Conservation Council, a group appointed by Mayor Richard J. Daley to supervise the neighborhood's redevelopment. In the meeting they began throwing chairs and yelling "down with urban renewal."[52]

The Chicago police came down hard on the YLO. They repeatedly arrested and jailed its leaders, including Jimenez, on minor infractions. In 1975, Jimenez moved from protests to politics and decided to take on the city's Democratic political machine. He ran for alderman of the Forty-Sixth Ward against a strong machine candidate. Jimenez was badly beaten and only garnered 27 percent of the vote. After Jimenez's defeat, the YLO disappeared by the mid-1970s. From 1963 to 1981, about seventeen Latino candidates ran for state and local offices. Only four won, all with the backing from the regular Democratic organization. The others, who ran as independents, lost by wide margins. They experienced a low Latino voter turnout, a shortage of funds, too few campaign workers and, of course, the muscle of the Democratic organization working against them.[53] Latinos did not yet have the political know-how and resources to beat the machine.

Division Street Riot

One event that awakened the political consciousness of Puerto Ricans was a riot that occurred in West Town and Humboldt Park on June 12, 1966. Historian Roger Biles noted that "Squeezed into a small area on the city's Near Northwest Side, the Puerto Ricans maintained a nearly invisible presence in Chicago. Although they endured the same discrimination and harsh living conditions as did Chicago's black population, the Puerto Ricans small numbers and corresponding lack of political influence made them easy to ignore—until June 12."[54] On that hot summer day, Puerto Ricans happily celebrated their first festive ethnic parade in downtown Chicago.

But by evening, things got ugly. A twenty-year-old man was involved in a street fight near Division Street and Damen Avenue, and police shot him in the leg. Police claimed he was armed, witnesses said he was not. More police were called in including police canine units. A large crowd refused to disperse. Allegedly a police officer allowed his German Shepherd dog to bite a man on the leg. For Puerto Ricans, the dogs symbolized all their hurts, real or imagined. The crowd of over four thousand, many teenagers, attacked the police. They pelted police with rocks, bottles, and cans. They smashed the windows of police cars, set two police cars on fire, and overturned another police car. Fifty-eight police squad cars arrived on the scene. More than a hundred police using tear gas and swinging their night sticks tried to disperse the crowd. Six additional police canine units with dozens of dogs were brought in. The sight of the large dogs only further enraged the crowd.[55] Puerto Ricans rioted the next day and a third day. Large crowds attacked and looted White-owned stores. Mayor Richard J. Daley was tempted to call out the Illinois National Guard for assistance. Finally, police restored peace. All told, sixteen people were injured, forty-nine arrested, and about fifty buildings were destroyed. Mayor Daley and city leaders were shocked that Puerto Ricans had rioted. The riot dispelled Daley's notion that Latinos were gullible or docile.

Chicago's Human Relations Commission held two days of public hearings to determine the causes of the riot. Puerto Rican speakers complained about abusive police, lack of jobs, bad housing, poor education, union discrimination, and poor city services. Yet the Commission's final written report, and editorials in the major newspapers, blamed the problems of Puerto Ricans on their inability to speak English and rapidly adjust in a new city.[56] Reporter Mike Royko wrote that "The causes were obvious: the usual job and housing discrimination, coupled with the city's indifference and the police habitual harshness. But Daley promptly blamed the trouble on 'outsiders.' He hadn't learned a thing from it."[57]

After the riot, someone in the mayor's administration gave a brief speech to Puerto Rican residents at the San Juan Theater on Division Street. The individual said that Mayor Daley was seeking more cooperation between city agencies and "Spanish-speaking" residents; the mayor agreed to name a Spanish-speaking special assistant in his office.[58] Mayor Daley later met with some Puerto Rican community leaders at City Hall. Daley did appoint Claudio Flores, a respected Puerto Rican newspaper publisher to the Chicago Commission on Human Relations. Flores was a staunch Daley supporter and a member of Amigos for Daley. In 1970, Flores quit his post on the Human Relations Commission protesting the city's inaction on Latino hiring and creating a jobs program.[59]

A month after the Division Street riot, Black people rioted on the city's West Side between July 12 and 15, 1966. The riot began when city workers turned off fire hydrants in Lawndale where Black children had turned them on to seek relief from the one-hundred-degree heat. Tempers flared between firemen and residents, and burning, looting, and sniping took place.[60] Mayor Daley called for the Illinois National Guard, who finally restored order. During the riot, two African American people died, eighty people suffered injuries, and police arrested four hundred rioters. Property damage exceeded $2 million.[61] Mayor Daley once again blamed the media and outsiders for the riot.

Red Squad

Some residents in the Puerto Rican community were ashamed Puerto Ricans had rioted. They believed the riot would forever paint Puerto Ricans as violence-prone and troublemakers. But others believed the riot politicized and created a new spirit of militancy among Puerto Ricans. In fact, new community organizations and a new generation of Puerto Rican leaders emerged shortly after the riot. For instance, Mirta Ramirez and community leaders formed a neighborhood group called the Spanish Action Committee of Chicago (SACC). After the riot, SACC members, together with two hundred people, marched from Humboldt Park to City Hall demanding that Mayor Daley address the concerns of Puerto Ricans. "The mayor met with some people from our group who they thought were the leaders," said Ramirez. "The mayor coopted those leaders. Some got city jobs. He appointed a few Puerto Ricans to city commissions. Some appeared in the newspapers with the mayor. Some got a little city money for their social programs. The city established an Urban Progress Center on Division Street to provide services."[62]

Mayor Daley, however, viewed the community organizing efforts of Puerto Ricans and Mexicans—and other activist community groups—as a threat to his absolute political power and control of the city. He had his police department trample on the rights of citizens. The Chicago Police Department's

Intelligence Division, known as the infamous Red Squad, infiltrated SACC and employed undercover operatives, public smear campaigns, and contrived press releases to discredit SACC as a "Communist" group. Police embarked on a "divide and conquer" strategy and pitted Mirta Ramirez and her husband against other members. "I left SACC and the organization was discredited as a Communist group and fell apart," said Ramirez.[63]

In the 1970s, Chicago's American Civil Liberties Union sued the Chicago Police Department (CPD) for violating the constitutional rights of free assembly and free speech of numerous community groups. In 1981, the city paid $306,250 to groups and individuals who were illegally spied on by the Red Squad. In 1984, a federal jury found that CPD violated the constitutional rights of the SACC, and the group was awarded $60,000 in damages. As a result of various lawsuits, CPD entered into court consent decrees promising to curb surveillance of lawful activities by community, political, and religious organizations.[64] The Red Squad was eventually disbanded.

Daley's Legacy

Mayor Richard J. Daley died of a heart attack on December 20, 1976, at age seventy-four. About twenty-five thousand people walked past Daley's coffin at Nativity of Our Lord Church in Bridgeport during the nineteen-hour wake. Authors Adam Cohen and Elizabeth Taylor summarized Daley's mixed legacy. They explained that many Chicagoans appreciated the positive things the mayor had accomplished: "He gave them jobs, stood up for their way of life against threats from all sides, and made their city work. He had built up Chicago, leaving skyscrapers, schools, highways, and a thriving downtown to proclaim his greatness."[65] However, other Chicagoans, the authors noted, remembered the negative aspects of Daley's career: "They viewed him as the master of a corrupt political system, backward-looking, power-hungry, and bigoted, who ruled in the name of some groups and at the expense of others. They saw him as someone who had built a city founded on unfairness, and who was deaf to calls for change."[66]

Despite the fact that Daley did very little to help Latinos achieve any kind of political power, he was immensely popular with Latinos, especially older, first-generation Latinos. Many Latinos, who traditionally voted for Democratic candidates, regularly voted for Mayor Daley and White machine candidates. Groups like Amigos for Daley held banquets and fund raisers for the mayor. Latinos seemed grateful that the mayor attended their ethnic parades and celebrations, and they asked for little in return.

However, things changed with younger, second-generation Latinos who, during the 1960s and '70s saw Mayor Daley and White old-guard politicians as a hindrance to their political progress. In 1966, young Puerto Ricans rioted on Division Street for three days protesting police brutality and demanding that city officials address the problems of poor housing, unemployment, and the lack of Latinos in city jobs. In the 1970s, groups like the Young Lords Organization protested Daley's plans for the gentrification of Lincoln Park, which had a sizable Puerto Rican community.

Younger Chicano activists also complained during the 1970s about White politicians who ignored the problems of their neighborhoods. They too engaged in protests and demonstrations in an effort to make city officials improve the schools, housing, and city services in their neighborhoods. There was a political awakening and many of these younger Latinos would lead the way in the struggle to acquire a voice in city politics.

CHAPTER TWO

Michael A. Bilandic and Jane M. Byrne— Same Old Thing?

Mayor Michael A. Bilandic: It's Snowing

After Richard J. Daley's death, there was a wild scramble for the mayor's seat. African Americans supported the African American Thirty-Fourth Ward alderman Wilson Frost. As the City Council's president pro tempore, African Americans believed Frost was entitled to be acting mayor. Most White aldermen were not ready to have an African American man as mayor. They changed the locks to the mayor's office to keep Frost shut out. Roman C. Pucinski, a prominent Polish Northwest Side alderman, pushed his candidacy, as did tough, Southeast Side, Tenth Ward alderman Edward "Fast Eddie" Vrdolyak. After several days of contentious negotiations in backrooms, the contestants agreed on a temporary mayor, Eleventh Ward alderman Michael A. Bilandic.[1]

Frost, Pucinski, and Vrdolyak were given consolation prizes. Frost was made chairman of the powerful City Council Finance Committee. Pucinski was given the position of vice mayor, a position without much formal authority. Vrdolyak was made council president pro tempore. The selection of Bilandic, who was Croatian, symbolized the weakening of Irish control in machine politics and the bestowing of beneficial status for Eastern European ethnics.[2] Bilandic was a lifelong resident of Bridgeport and had served as Daley's surrogate in the City Council since 1969. Shortly after becoming interim mayor, Bilandic reneged on his earlier promise to not run in the special election for mayor; he announced his candidacy in the special election.

In less than two years in office, Bilandic had an undistinguished career and produced few changes in City Hall. "Michael Bilandic is most remembered for how he entered and exited office and not for what he accomplished as the city's chief executive," wrote Paul M. Green.[3] Like Mayor Daley, Bilandic viewed African American and Latino voters as unimportant, marginal players in Chicago politics. Bilandic had to realize Latinos were a growing population eager for a political voice in city affairs. By 1970, the US Census counted "nearly 250,000 persons of Spanish language in Chicago. By 1977, it was estimated that the population had more than doubled. Of the estimated 500,000 persons of Spanish language in the city, 72,596 are registered to vote, comprising 4.5 percent of the city's electorate."[4] Yet Bilandic did not appoint any Latinos to high-ranking positions in his administration. He did not extend any assistance to help Latinos win elected office.

Ben Joravsky, political reporter for the *Chicago Reader* said, "Mayor Bilandic ignored Latinos. He didn't do anything for them. Bilandic was a continuation of the same old policies of the Democratic machine. . . . I think it just had to do with prejudice that some white people have toward Hispanics. And the fact that Latinos were the new kids on the block. White politicians were going to take care of their people."[5] Bilandic catered largely to the concerns of the city's White ethnic groups. He did not seem to care that the racial and ethnic composition in Chicago had changed dramatically. He probably thought the political machine was invincible and would go on ruling the city forever. "The old pols had been lulled and misled by the ease of the Bilandic appointment. Their fight to retain power would never again go unchallenged," wrote Green.[6]

Many believe Bilandic lost the election in 1979 mainly because of a series of blunders during the January 1979 snow blizzard. Cars and trucks were stranded throughout the city, preventing snowplows and salt trucks from doing their work. Mayor Bilandic announced a snow-removal plan that was ineffective but had cost the city $90,000. He angered the city's African American community when Chicago Transit Authority trains going into the city's downtown business district, the Loop, did not make scheduled stops at predominately African American stations. As a result, African American commuters could not get to their downtown jobs. Yet the trains continued making regular stops at White stations where commuters were not inconvenienced.[7] It was not just the city's poor response to the snow blizzard that angered voters. Writer Michael B. Preston argued that many Chicagoans including, "White voters were dissatisfied with the Bilandic administration over the breakdown in city services [i.e. snow removal] cronyism in city government, corruption, and the apparent condoning of the condominium hustle by real estate interests that tended to drive up rents. This combination of factors led to Bilandic's defeat."[8]

Mayor Richard J. Daley had appointed Jane M. Byrne as the city's first commissioner of the Department of Consumer Sales, Weights, and Measures. She was a loyal Daley follower and with Daley's sponsorship she became a member of the Democratic National committee and cochairman of the Cook County Democratic Central Committee. As commissioner, Byrne publicly accused Mayor Bilandic of corruption by "greasing" the way for a taxi-fare increase. Bilandic vehemently denied the charge. A grand jury found no evidence of wrongdoing on Mayor Bilandic's part.[9] Bilandic unceremoniously fired Byrne on November 21, 1977. Byrne then decided to run for mayor against Bilandic. Very few people believed she could win.

Mayor Jane M. Byrne: "The Evil Cabal"

Jane M. Byrne announced her candidacy for mayor on April 24, 1978, ten months before the Democratic primary. She held a press conference and read her "declaration of candidacy." She portrayed herself as an anti-machine reformer and said, "that City Hall had fallen into the clutches of a 'cabal of evil men.' She said the evil men included Bilandic, and Aldermen Eddie Burke and Eddie Vrdolyak and others."[10] At her press conference she said, "These sinister apostles of self-aggrandizement not only present a clear and present danger to good government, but they threaten to perpetuate themselves in the seats of the mighty and I believe present a menace that calls for a united response from the citizens of Chicago."[11]

The Democratic primary was held on February 27, 1979. Bilandic received strong support from the South Side's White ethnics and won more Latino votes than Byrne.[12] But Byrne had strong support from the African American wards. Chicago's major newspapers had endorsed Bilandic. Byrne received 51 percent of the vote in one of the most stunning upsets in Chicago history.[13] Byrne received 412,909 votes and Bilandic received 396,134 votes. She made history as the city's first female mayor. "On the evening of her Democratic primary win over Bilandic, Jane Byrne shouted to her family and friends gathered in her hotel suite, "I beat the whole goddamn Machine, single-handed."[14]

Those who voted for Jane M. Byrne—White people, progressives, African Americans, Latinos, and women—saw her as independent and progressive with new ideas for governing the city. But they were soon disillusioned by her actions during her first weeks in office. She quickly saw herself as the new "boss" of the Daley political machine. Old-guard machine aldermen found the new mayor most accommodating. According to Melvin G. Holli, "Mayor Jane's masterful inaction let the machine politicians and the 'evil cabal,' led by councilmen Edward 'Fast Eddie' Vrdolyak and Edward Burke, to organize the council committees and select their chairmen. Oberman and the reformers had been left out in the cold seemingly without influence. The hopes for political reform died at the starting gate."[15]

Don Rose, who was Byrne's campaign manager, and had helped engineer her mayoral victory, became estranged from Byrne after just one year. Jane M. Byrne denied that she sided with the "evil cabal." In her memoir Byrne said, "I did not 'side with the evil cabal,' as some people charged, but I practiced the art of compromise, without ever making improper or underhanded deals. It's harder to walk a tightrope than to engage in a slugfest, but it gets you somewhere."[16]

Calamity Jane

Shortly after assuming office, Mayor Jane M. Byrne encountered problems with the city's major labor unions. In December 1979, she challenged the demands of the transit union, and the union threatened to strike during the Christmas shopping season. Chicago's downtown business community pressured the administration and the union to settle. The union returned to work.[17] In January 1980, the teachers' union went out on strike to try and win back certain jobs it had bargained away in the fall 1979 school talks between the Chicago Teachers Union and the city. The teachers struck for two weeks. Then on February 14, Chicago firefighters went out on strike over the lack of a union contract promised by Mayor Byrne. The strike dragged on for twenty-three days. Byrne did not handle the strikes very well. In negotiations with the three unions she appeared to be controlling, vindictive, and mean. Reporters and union leaders poked fun at Byrne by referring to her as "Attila the Hen" or "Calamity Jane."[18] Under Byrne, there seemed to be a major labor strike almost once a month. Many Chicagoans were angered by Byrne's lack of leadership and her inability to win labor peace with the city's major labor unions.

Confrontation Politics

During the Democratic primary for mayor, many volunteers came flocking to Byrne's headquarters. One volunteer who called Byrne's headquarters was Elena Martinez. She had left Cuba in 1961 after the Bay of Pigs invasion. When Byrne picked up the phone and heard Elena's Spanish accent, she was elated.

Byrne needed a spokesperson to help win over the Latino vote and Elena seemed perfect for the job.[19] Martinez worked hard for Byrne, working weekends, evenings, and nights. She was answering phones and scheduling appearances. Byrne and Martinez worked closely together and seemed to enjoy each other's company. Byrne told Martinez that there would be a job for her in her administration after the election.

On March 8, 1979, nine days after the primary that Byrne won, Elena Martinez gave Byrne a memo outlining several issues the Latino community wanted her to address when she became mayor. The memo was apparently given to Martinez by a community organization called the West Town Concerned Citizens Coalition (WTCCC). The WTCCC was a Puerto Rican activist group in the Humboldt Park community that used protests to get the attention of elected officials. The issues in the memo concerned bilingual education and the hiring of Latinos in the police and fire departments and in key cabinet positions. Byrne, however, had not responded to the memo, and Martinez no longer had easy access to Byrne like before.[20] Two weeks later, Martinez ran into Byrne in the hallway and inquired about her position regarding the memo. Obviously angry, "Jane grabbed the memo from Elena, stabbing the paper with her fingernail, and said, 'I'm not going to answer this. Just look at these. The Latinos did not vote for me, and I spent all that money there. I'll answer these when I'm good and ready.'"[21]

On March 23, ten days before the regular election, members of the WTCCC picketed Byrne's office. They then barged into Byrne's office demanding to know what she intended to do for the Latinos, and why they should support her. According to writer Kathleen Whalen FitzGerald, "Elena stood next to Jane, while the Latinos filled her small office. It was an angry confrontation. The Latinos were tired of being used. Jane looked to Elena, her cochairman of Latinos for Byrne, to respond to her own people."[22] The WTCCC members asked Martinez, in Spanish, not to say anything. They wanted Byrne to answer their demands. The group coerced promises from Byrne regarding the issues they raised, but later as mayor, she did not honor any of her promises. Byrne now perceived Martinez as disloyal and not someone she could depend on. Byrne would not offer Martinez a well-paying, visible position in her mayoral administration.[23] Martinez received nothing for all her hard work on behalf of Byrne.

Mayor Byrne soon earned the reputation of a person who demanded strict loyalty from others but was loyal to very few. She was viewed as a person who did not keep her word. Writer Eugene Kennedy said, "Politics works, so the veterans say, only because at some level you keep your word. That is the glue that makes government work. Mayor Daley said little and kept the words he gave. Jane Byrne says a lot, but her critics feel that she does not keep her word."[24] There would be other confrontations between the WTCCC and Byrne after she became mayor. Reverend Jorge Morales was president of the WTCCC during the 1970s and '80s. "We were a thorn in the side of Mayor Jane Byrne," said Morales. "We held several noisy demonstrations against the city and the Chicago post office over the lack of Latino employees. We pressured the city to fix schools, clean neighborhoods, and provide more city services. Those things were important to our community."[25]

Latino Appointments

Although Jane M. Byrne was the new mayor, Latinos still found themselves powerless. As loyal Democrats, Latinos had voted for Byrne, yet, like previous mayors, she was not reaching out to them. No Latino served on Byrne's transition team. Byrne was afraid that Richard M. Daley would challenge her for the mayor's seat in the 1983 election, so she made a calculated attempt to try and win over White ethnic constituents to the exclusion of Latinos and African Americans. William J. Grimshaw said that "Time and time again she pitted black against white ethnic representation—in school, police, public housing, and ward boundary disputes—and came down heavily on the white ethnic side."[26] In her first year in office, Byrne helped Carmen Velásquez become a member of the Chicago Board of Education. But soon after, Byrne dumped Velásquez. Byrne angered Latinos and African Americans by replacing them and putting White people on the school board. In 1979, Byrne had won praise for appointing a majority African American and ethnic minority school board. In 1980, however, she again angered the African American community by dumping two African American members of the Chicago Board of Education and replacing them with White opponents of busing.[27]

Byrne was under pressure from community groups to appoint some Latinos to her administration. Yet Byrne's only Latino appointment during her first year was Dr. Hugo H. Muriel, a Bolivian-born physician, as commissioner of the Chicago Department of Public Health. Muriel was the mayor's personal doctor and family friend. He was the first Latino named to a top city post. Many Latinos became upset with the Muriel appointment. He was Bolivian, they argued, and not from the two major Latino groups in Chicago—Mexicans and Puerto Ricans. He had no previous community contacts with Latinos. And he was a specialist in endocrinology and had no medical expertise in public health. A week after Dr. Muriel's appointment, Latinos occupied the mayor's offices. They demanded that the mayor explain what she planned to do for Latinos regarding patronage jobs, neighborhood development funds, and better police work with neighborhood gangs. The mayor made a presentation to a local community group, where she promised to seek federal money to help invest in a Latino neighborhood. One year later, none of the mayor's promises had been fulfilled.[28]

Mayor Byrne did appoint Raul Villalobos as president of the Chicago Board of Education. She also gave a city job to Angel Correa, a twenty-four-year-old, who worked in her campaign gathering signatures for her nominating petitions. Byrne rewarded him with a $35,000-a-year city job as deputy commissioner in her newly created Department of Neighborhoods.[29] It was unclear what Correa's job responsibilities were. Many assumed it was simply an old-fashioned, do-very-little-work patronage job. Mayor Byrne earned the reputation of having a revolving door administration. Department heads and mayoral staff would come and go very quickly. Most of her appointments came from the North Side Irish community. She had very few women or African Americans in her administration. One of her Latino appointments to the Police Board, a former campaign aide, became an embarrassment when it was reported that he was wearing a gun entering the mayor's office.[30]

While Byrne had very few Latinos in her administration, she was able to appoint her husband, Jay McMullen, as her press secretary and political adviser. She argued the appointment was not nepotism because he was paid only a dollar a year. She explained that "The rest of his salary—it was a secret— would come out of her secret political fund. . . . Jay, for his part, lost no time in affecting the image of Rasputin in turtleneck sweaters. He threatened to 'bloody noses' of those who criticized his wife."[31]

Hacienda Politics

In 1981, community members in Humboldt Park and West Town formed a new group called the Political Action Organization (PAO) to study reapportionment and discuss the future of Latino politics. Another Humboldt Park group, Latinos for Political Progress (LPP), which began in 1971, was also looking at reapportionment. "We want to exercise our political voice to make sure we are represented," said John Alvarez, a self-employed businessman who chaired the redistricting committees of both PAO and LPP. "Ten years ago Latinos did not know what redistricting was."[32] Aracelis Figueroa, a principal at Avondale elementary school, ran a spirited, independent campaign for alderman in the Thirty-First Ward in 1979. Although she pulled 4,691 votes, it was not enough to beat the machine candidate, Chester B. Kuta, who won with 7,632 votes. Figueroa said, "I spent $37,000 and $17,000 of it my own, and I had enough staff, but it was mainly voter fraud by the Democratic machine that caused us to lose."[33]

As the mayoral election of 1983 got closer, Mayor Jane M. Byrne started to aggressively court the Latino vote. She started going to dinners, ethnic parades, and other functions in the Latino communities. Sometimes, she showed up uninvited and made herself the center of attention. She pledged $5,000 to LPP. "Mayor Byrne recognizes the importance of the Hispanic vote," said Edward M. Burke, powerful alderman of the Fourteenth Ward. "She's playing smart politics by courting Hispanics. Whoever can harness the Hispanic vote can be politically powerful."[34] Byrne was not going to wait for Latino community groups to pick their independent, progressive Latino candidates to run for office. She wanted to pick her own loyal Latino machine politician. The mayor, working closely with Thomas E. Keane, convinced Chester Kuta to step down as Thirty-First Ward alderman. He was given a city job at double his aldermanic salary. Then, on December 11, 1981, Mayor Byrne handpicked Joseph José Martinez, Puerto Rican, as alderman of the Thirty-First Ward. Martinez had firm roots in the regular Democratic Organization. He was formerly a precinct captain in the Thirty-First Ward and an attorney in the law firm of Edward M. Burke.[35]

Mayor Byrne hoped the Martinez appointment would please Puerto Ricans. Instead, it enraged many Puerto Ricans who argued that the mayor was engaging in "hacienda politics," where outsiders handpicked politicians who were loyal to the machine and placed them in Latino neighborhoods. In the African American community they called this "plantation politics." Martinez, some community leaders claimed, had no record of neighborhood involvement. They argued that Thomas E. Keane would continue to control the ward through Martinez. "The very first time I voted, it was for Mayor Jane Byrne," said former state Senator Miguel del Valle. "But I quickly became disappointed with Byrne. . . . I thought the Martinez appointment was an insult. We had evolved from having non-Latino representation that was totally disconnected. Then we had the same politicians, who had all the power, now determine what Latino would represent us."[36]

Martinez did not last long as alderman. Edward Nedza, a machine loyalist, was state Senator of the Fifth District on the Northwest Side. He was also the committeeman of the Thirty-First Ward. Nedza was not pleased with the Martinez appointment; he wanted a Puerto Rican alderman he could control. Nedza maneuvered behind the scenes to get Martinez out and get his guy in. In 1983, Martinez announced that he would not seek reelection. He got a position with the city's cable commission. Nedza slated Miguel Santiago, a schoolteacher and precinct captain.

Santiago won the 1983 election without difficulty. Author Milton Rakove predicted in the early 1980s that, "The Democratic machine will try to buy off the rising Latino leadership. And future Latino politicians may put their political interests before any Latino community interest."[37] Chicago aldermen have a reputation for sometimes doing and saying outrageous things. Santiago quickly added to the reputation. Shortly after Harold Washington won the 1983 general election, Santiago tried to embarrass the new mayor. Santiago called his first press conference to say a community activist, an ally of the mayor, had threatened to set his feet on fire. Peter Earle, the community activist, explained that he had only told Santiago that he would be held accountable by the community, and "we're going to hold your feet to the fire."[38] Santiago was ridiculed because he did not have a firm understanding of English.

Fighting Back

The Mexican American Legal Defense and Educational Fund (MALDEF) is a dynamic civil rights organization that was founded in San Antonio, Texas, in 1968. The organization successfully fought in the courts—especially in the Southwest—against discrimination of Mexicans in education, employment, voting rights, and public services. The organization had offices in San Antonio, San Francisco, Los Angeles, Washington, DC, and Denver. In October of 1980, MALDEF decided to open a regional office in Chicago. By 1980, Latinos represented 14 percent of Chicago's three-million-person population, and 5.5 percent of Illinois's population. Yet Latinos lacked any political representation in Chicago or Illinois. MALDEF's small group of young, energetic lawyers, like Virginia Martinez and Ray Romero, quickly turned their attention to the issue of political empowerment for Latinos.

The Illinois State Legislature had failed to adopt a redistricting plan by June 30, 1981, as mandated under the 1970 Illinois Constitution. As a result, in July 1981, the Legislative Redistricting Commission ("Commission") was established. Immediately, there was concern among the Latino community because the Commission had no Latino representation, and they worried that their communities might be gerrymandered. The Commission adopted a new redistricting plan in October 1981.[39] In 1982, MALDEF and Latino voters, and African American plaintiffs challenged the redistricting plan adopted by the Commission. Miguel del Valle, then working in social services, became a plaintiff in the legal case. According to attorney Patricia Mendoza, who wrote about the case, "The Del Valle plaintiffs alleged that although those responsible for drawing district lines for Chicago were aware of these sizable Hispanic population centers, [they] intentionally fractured [split up] both Hispanic communities by dividing each community among four separate legislative districts."[40]

The parties reached a settlement on January 7, 1982, and the court upheld the settlement. "We had worked with a number of Latino community organizations and we had agreement on the map that we were going to put forward. We won the case. [Then in the settlement] we were trying to work out how the district lines were going to be changed to accommodate us as well as African Americans, who won their case," said Virginia Martinez, lead attorney for MALDEF in the state and city wards lawsuits.[41] In the settlement, Latinos were now about 71 percent of the population in Illinois House District 20, about 63 percent in House District 9, and 50 percent in House District Ten and 56 percent in Senate District Five. Therefore, the first Latino state legislative districts were established.[42]

After the settlement, in 1983, the first Latino state Representative elected was Joseph Berrios in the Ninth District. In 1984, Juan Soliz won in the Twentieth District. Miguel del Valle was elected as the first Latino state senator in 1987. "The lawsuit was historically significant in helping Latinos achieve political power at the state level, absolutely," said Martinez.[43] Some in the Latino community were not pleased that Joseph Berrios—who they saw as part of the Democratic political machine—won. "We were going to have the opportunity to elect an independent, Latino state representative in the Ninth

District," said Miguel del Valle. "We selected Jose Salgado as our candidate. But we botched Salgado's petitions. The Chicago Board of Elections Commissioners disqualified him from the ballot because of an insufficient number of valid signatures. We didn't know what we were doing. Berrios ran opposed and won."[44]

MALDEF also contested how majority Latino city wards were redrawn. Mayor Byrne brought back former alderman Thomas E. Keane to help her redraw city wards after the 1980 census. In 1981, the City Council adopted a ward map that provided for four Hispanic wards. This seemed to be a victory for the Latino community, which had never before had a majority ward.[45] But Latinos rejected the adopted map because it defined a Latino ward as one with a simple majority of more than 50 percent. Latino voters, however, argued that a simple majority of Latinos in a ward was insufficient to allow Latinos to elect a candidate of their choice. They wanted wards with at least a 65 percent Latino population.[46] In the summer of 1982, MALDEF, together with the New York–based Puerto Rican Legal Defense and Education Fund and James P. Chapman and Associates, filed suit on behalf of six Latino voters, called the Velasco plaintiffs. Two other groups of plaintiffs, including African Americans, also filed suit, and the three suits were consolidated as *Ketchum v. Byrne*. African American and Latino plaintiffs argued that the City Council map violated the federal Voting Rights Act of 1965 and was drawn deliberately to dilute the voting strength of minority voters.

Latino plaintiffs wanted new wards with a 65 percent Latino population to account for the fact that the voting age population was younger in Latino wards, their voter registration and turnout was lower and some residents were ineligible to vote because they were not US citizens. "This was a deliberate attempt to gerrymander and disenfranchise Latinos. Absolutely. White aldermen in the City Council were opposed to our lawsuit. Nobody gives up power. Nobody was going to say, 'Okay, I'll give up my ward and you can have it as a Latino ward.' Several White aldermen testified in court and said I get along with the Latino community. Alderman Richard Mell [Thirty-Third Ward], said, 'I love Puerto Ricans,'" said Virginia Martinez.[47]

Mayor Byrne, alderman Edward Vrdolyak of the Tenth Ward, and other machine politicians spent over a million dollars of taxpayer money and time defending their map. The District Court agreed with the City Council that a simple majority was enough to permit a minority group to elect a candidate of its choice. The plaintiffs disagreed and appealed to the appellate court.

Federal Judge Thomas McMillan overturned the city map and ordered that a new map be drawn. The plaintiffs claimed that the McMillan map did not move far enough to remedy past discrimination.[48] They continued their legal challenge. The court of appeals agreed with the plaintiffs that "supermajorities" of 65 percent minority population should be created, and it sent the case back to the district court with specific guidelines on how to come up with a more equitable map in three African American wards and four Latino wards.

Under Vrdolyak's leadership, the city, as defendants, took the case all the way to the US Supreme Court. However, in June 1985, the high court upheld the appellate court by declining to hear an appeal.[49] In 1985, the parties presented a new settlement map to the court for approval, which created four majority Latino wards with greater percentages of Latino voting age population than the originally challenged map.[50] At the end of 1985, Judge Charles Norgle Sr. accepted the new map. The number of African American voters was also increased in the three African American wards. In a brilliant legal move, the plaintiffs also asked the court that special elections soon take place in the city wards that were redrawn under the settlement plan. Machine politicians vehemently opposed any special elections. But the court granted the request. The special ward elections took place on March 16, 1986. "The city ward lawsuit was historically significant. It was a major signal to the powers-that-be that we weren't going to stay silent anymore," said Virginia Martinez. "We had an organization and resources to be able to fight. The special ward elections also gave the one vote majority in the City Council to the new Black mayor Harold Washington. It finally ended the Council Wars."[51]

Disorderly Conduct Arrests

Mayor Byrne, like her mentor, Richard J. Daley, used the Chicago Police Department (CPD) to violate the constitutional rights of some minority citizens. In the early 1980s, a *Chicago Reporter* investigation found that under the Byrne administration, police were making approximately 150,000 "disorderly conduct" arrests each year, predominately in African American and Latino neighborhoods. What constituted disorderly conduct arrests was often vague, and few cases were prosecuted because officers routinely failed to show up in court. It appeared Mayor Byrne and the police were using the arrests of mostly young males as a way to control the gang problem in the city.[52] The American Civil Liberties Union (ACLU) used the *Chicago Reporter* investigation to file a lawsuit against the CPD. An angry federal judge declared the practice unconstitutional after city officials repeatedly failed to show up in court to defend themselves. As part of its order, the court directed the city to expunge more than 800,000 disorderly arrests over the prior five years where the arresting officer failed to appear for court hearings. By the early 1990s, disorderly conduct arrests dropped to approximately 60,000 per year.[53]

Illegal "Aliens"

Jane M. Byrne was not very pleased when Harold Washington beat her and Richard M. Daley in 1983 to become the city's first African American mayor. She wanted her old job back and all of the perks that came with it. Byrne and Daley had split the White vote and she did not want that to happen again. So she announced her candidacy nearly two years in advance of the 1987 Democratic mayoral primary. She wanted to be the sole White candidate to challenge Washington. She campaigned heavily in White ethnic and Latino wards. She began showing up regularly at Latino community events, again, sometimes uninvited. She reminded Latino residents of the many good things she did for them, such as appointing the first Latino alderman. Mayor Washington, for his part, kept reminding Latinos it was Byrne who drew up the city ward map that gerrymandered Latino and African American wards. Byrne even learned a few Spanish words. She offered to debate Washington on a Spanish-language television. The mayor ridiculed her, "She can't use English; how does she expect to try Spanish?"[54]

At one campaign stop on Chicago's South Side, Byrne made a serious blunder. She announced her plan for a crackdown on drugs. She said Chicago's population had been growing from an influx of "alien" immigration of Cambodians, Laotians, Koreans, and Puerto Ricans. Byrne obviously did not know that Puerto Ricans are US citizens by birth. Many Puerto Ricans were offended. A political button was quickly created with the message: "I am not an Alien, Jane. I'm a Human Being for Harold Washington." Byrne did receive some Latino votes. But a larger percentage of Latinos voted for Harold Washington and he beat Byrne in the 1987 primary. Byrne did not run for political office again. Chicago decided to create a memorial to formally recognize Byrne. In August 2014, the confluence of the Kennedy, Dan Ryan, and Eisenhower expressways and the Ida B. Well Drive, was dedicated as the "Jane M. Byrne Interchange."[55]

Many of the people who voted for Jane M. Byrne when she first ran for mayor in 1979—White people, African Americans, and Latinos—saw her as an independent, progressive person who would reform city politics. But they were soon disappointed when she became close friends with old-guard, machine politicians and started acting like a "boss." Latinos were especially angered by many of the things Byrne did that hurt their community. For instance, she had only a few Latinos in her administration. Just like in the Richard J. Daley era, Latinos received very few city jobs. They also received very few city business contracts. When repeatedly confronted by activist community groups, Byrne promised she would fix Latino neighborhoods and provide better city services; and then she would do very little or nothing. Byrne enraged Puerto Ricans when she handpicked Joseph José Martinez as alderman of the Thirty-First Ward. Puerto Ricans found it insulting that she was trying to dictate who their political leaders should be.

Latinos also had to challenge Byrne and old-guard, machine politicians in the courts when they tried to gerrymander four Latino city wards and three Black wards. It was a costly and time-consuming fight but ultimately the courts agreed that the population numbers in the four Latino wards and three African American wards had to increase significantly. The courts also ordered special elections in the seven redrawn wards. Byrne also had the Chicago Police Department engage in making mass disorderly conduct arrests of young African American and Latino males as a way of trying to deal with the city's gang problem. The courts declared the arrests as unconstitutional. And finally, Byrne insulted Puerto Ricans when she referred to them as "aliens."

CHAPTER THREE

Harold Washington and Reform

arold Washington was once part of Chicago's political machine. He worked with his father, Roy, a precinct worker, as his assistant in various campaigns. William J. Grimshaw noted that "The organizational bond did not form until after his father's death in 1953. He joined the Third Ward Democratic organization in the fall of 1954, taking over his father's precinct and inheriting his city job in the Corporation Counsel's Office."[1] He worked for the Democratic organization for many years. Later, Washington was elected to the Illinois Legislature in 1965 and served through 1978. He then served in the United States Congress for two terms.

During the Great Migration, from 1916 to 1970, about six million African Americans relocated from the South to northern cities. Thousands of these migrants came to Chicago and looked to the political machine for favors, especially jobs. These early arrivals were mainly poor, uneducated, and lacked political experience. This made it easy for political machines in northern cities like Chicago to take advantage of them.[2] They were a controlled vote and very loyal to Chicago's political machine. Precinct captains dispensed favors for votes at election time: giving people turkeys, garbage cans, fixing parking tickets, and offering them a few low-level patronage jobs. Consequently, African Americans usually voted for Mayor Richard J. Daley and other White politicians. The six African America aldermen serving on the Chicago City Council in the mid-1960s were known as the "Silent Six" because they rarely spoke up to challenge Mayor Daley.[3]

But by the early 1960s, many African Americans became increasingly disillusioned with Mayor Daley and his political machine. An African American independent movement was forming in Chicago. According to political organizer Don Rose, "Chicago's independent black political movement really began in 1963, in the heat of the civil rights battle over schools, when a group of eight independent black candidates ran for City Council."[4] By the early 1970s,

African American disappointment with the political machine had reached a crescendo. Many African Americans, including Washington, saw the political machine as a hindrance to their political future. Under Mayor Richard J. Daley, African Americans—just like Latinos—were not offered well-paying city jobs despite their loyalty to his machine. Top party and government positions were reserved for the mayor's Irish friends, neighbors, and family. While African American wards regularly produced large voter turnouts for Mayor Daley and White machine candidates, their votes were taken for granted.[5]

African Americans also saw that under Mayor Daley, they received inferior city services and little economic investment in their neighborhoods. Their schools and neighborhoods were still highly segregated, and city officials were not seriously addressing the constant problem of police brutality in their communities. In fact, Washington became so disillusioned with the political machine that he decided to challenge it. He ran for mayor in 1977 in a special election to replace Richard J. Daley, who died while in office. He ran against Michael Bilandic. He did poorly and did not get a huge African American vote although he did win some of the African American wards. Washington was not too disappointed that he lost; he had gained valuable experience on how to run a mayoral campaign. "This was typical of what was happening in cities throughout the country," wrote Don Rose. "There was usually a trial run, with the black mayoral candidate losing, but the next time out, a black would win, as occurred in Newark and Detroit."[6]

Coalition Politics

During Jane M. Byrne's one term as mayor, she managed to repeatedly insult and anger African Americans. The assault by Byrne on African American interests occurred in three critical arenas, argued William J. Grimshaw: "In the city council, where the boundary lines of a new ward map eliminated black majorities in three wards (and Hispanic majorities in four wards), and in the public schools and public housing, two majority-black institutions, where black leadership was reduced by Byrne."[7] Washington once said, "Politics is like shooting pool or eating Cracker Jacks. Once you start you just can't stop."[8] And he certainly couldn't stop. He was persuaded by African American community leaders to throw his hat in the ring in the 1983 mayoral race. In the primary, the media did not take his candidacy seriously. He was not given much of a chance of winning the election. The real showdown, the media and public believed, was between the two Irish heavyweights, Jane M. Byrne and Richard M. Daley. Daley won the endorsement of the city's major newspapers. Byrne was building huge leads in the public opinion polls.

Washington ran on a reform platform; he criticized the ways of the old political machine. He pledged to open up access to city government and to be fair to all Chicago residents. Washington was seen both as a reform mayor and messiah in the African American community.[9] His mayoral campaign soon took on the characteristics of a social movement. A registration drive added about 125,000 new African American voters to the rolls. Washington realized that to win the mayor's seat he would have to appeal to a larger audience of potential voters besides African Americans; he would have to appeal to progressive White people and Latinos. Washington engaged in coalition building and in creating a rainbow coalition. Washington campaigned strongly in White lakefront liberal wards. Moreover, he wisely courted the city's growing Latino community by campaigning in Mexican and Puerto Rican wards. Writer Paul Kleppner argued that "Washington based his appeal to Hispanics on the experience of racial discrimination that they shared with blacks. He pointed to his support in Congress for bilingual education, pledged to work for the appointment of a Hispanic as district schools superintendent, and promised an affirmative action policy that would give Hispanics their appropriate share of city jobs."[10]

Rudy Lozano

In the 1980s in Chicago, Latino community activists turned their attention to the electoral politics as a way of obtaining civil rights and gaining empowerment for their communities.[11] One of the first Latinos to support Washington in his 1983 mayoral race was Rudy Lozano, an emerging, charismatic Mexican leader. In 1979, the young Lozano, who was a community activist and labor organizer, founded a group called Por Un Barrio Mejor (For a Better Neighborhood). The organization fought for the rights of immigrants and laborers. Lozano realized that Mexicans were outside the circle of power, looking in. "Rudy Lozano, other community activists, and I were against getting involved in electoral politics," said former state Senator Jesús "Chuy" García. "We thought it was corrupt. In 1977 we visited Springfield, Illinois attempting to kill anti-immigrant legislation. We discovered how powerless we were in electoral politics. While growing in numbers, we were voiceless and vote less in the City Council."[12]

Lozano and García concluded that participating in electoral politics was indeed a progressive way to empower Latinos. Lozano and García established the Twenty-Second Ward Independent Political Organization. The alderman of the Twenty-Second Ward, which includes Little Village, was Frank Stemberk, a quiet, loyal machine politico. Lozano and García discovered that Stemberk did not even live in the ward but in his main home in a western suburb. They leaked the story to a reporter who published it tarnishing Stemberk's reputation. In 1983, Lozano challenged Stemberk for alderman. The political machine put three other Latino candidates on the ballot to split the Mexican vote. Lozano lost a runoff vote against Stemberk by seventeen votes, and Stemberk won the election. Many Lozano supporters wondered if the political machine stole the aldermanic election by purging Latino voters from poll sheets shortly before the election. Lozano refused to legally contest the results of the election; instead he wanted to focus on helping Washington win the mayoral election.

Shortly after Washington won the election, Lozano, in his early thirties with two young children, was shot to death in his home in June 1983. Police convicted a young, Mexican gang member of his murder. Yet police angered the Mexican community by stating that the man acted alone. Police failed to establish a motive for the shooting. Lozano's family and supporters were convinced that others were involved in the killing. They believed Lozano's labor and political organizing activities were the motives for his killing.[13] Mexicans highly respected Lozano. Thousands of people walked in the streets while attending his funeral. Later, a Chicago Public Library branch and a public elementary school were named in Lozano's honor, and a book about his life—Rudy Lozano, His Life, His People—was published.[14] Lozano's campaign manager Jesús García decided to continue Lozano's political work.

García and other Mexican community leaders supported Washington in his bid for mayor. "We were glad Harold Washington was running for mayor," said García. "We had met and dealt with him in Springfield, Illinois in the mid-1970s. In Congress, he had championed immigrant rights and bilingual education. We told him if he ran for mayor, he would have allies working for him in the Latino community."[15]

A Hard-Won Victory

Across town in the predominately Puerto Rican wards, Miguel del Valle, Luis Gutiérrez, Reverend Jorge Morales, and other community leaders supported Washington and vigorously campaigned for him in the 1983 primary. Even though Washington was the most qualified of the three candidates running for office, many White people, and some Latinos—due to racial prejudice—simply refused to vote for him. The city was very racially divided. Mayor Jane M. Byrne's assistant press secretary for Spanish communication played on voters' racial fears by telling a Spanish-language television audience that Harold Washington would hire mostly Black people if he were elected mayor. He said, "We can go to the Department of Human Services, and we will see how dark that department is. Can you imagine how it would be with a mayor with a face of that color?"[16] The Midwest Voter Registration and Education Project's exit poll found that more than 66,000 Latinos, or 68.6 percent of those registered, turned out to vote in the Democratic primary. Of those interviewed, 12.7 percent said they voted for Harold Washington, 34.5 percent for Richard M. Daley, and 51.4 percent for Jane Byrne.[17] White ethnic voters split their votes between Byrne and Daley. In the Democratic primary, Washington won with 36 percent of the votes to Byrne's 34 percent and Daley's 30 percent.

Many lifelong White Democrats, refused to vote for Washington in the general election. Instead, they supported the Republican candidate, Bernard Epton. The racial code words of Epton's campaign were "Epton—Before It's Too Late." In other words, Epton was telling White voters to resist electing an African American person as mayor and instead vote for "the good White guy." On Palm Sunday, March 27, 1983, a crowd of Epton supporters jeered Washington and former Vice President Walter Mondale as they tried to attend religious services at St. Pascal's Roman Catholic Church on the city's Northwest Side. "The words 'NIGGER DIE' were freshly spray-painted on one of the doors to the church," said Paul Kleppner.[18] In the general election, the Washington camp redoubled their efforts to bring more Latinos into the campaign. According to María de los Angeles Torres, "Latinos were added to the Campaign Steering Committee. The Issues Committee, the Special Events Committee and the Press Committee hired Latino staff. Latino Operations was made part of precinct coordination. In precinct operations, two Latinos were hired to interface with the operations in the neighborhood."[19]

It was a close contest. Nevertheless, with over a million votes cast, Washington won the general election with 48,250 votes. He won 90 percent of African American votes, 17 percent of White votes, and 79 percent of more than 95,000 Latino votes. Washington won 79 percent of Puerto Rican votes, 68 percent of Mexican votes, 75 percent of Central and South American votes, and 54 percent of Cuban votes.[20] Latino voter turnout reached an all-time high. Many believed Latinos were the crucial "swing vote" that enabled Washington to win the election. "Folks around the country are watching to see if the Hispanic-black coalition works here," said Juan Andrade of the Midwest Voter and Registration Project. "We brought their man over the top. Harold acknowledged that himself. Now it's time to see if he's going to make winners out of us."[21] Chicago elected its first African American mayor but it had not been easy. While many African Americans celebrated Washington's victory, many White people were disappointed and angry that an African American was now the city's mayor. The mayoral contest exposed how the city was deeply racially divided.

Black and Brown Faces at City Hall

Washington immediately signed the Shakman court decree. The landmark antipatronage lawsuit was named after Michael Shakman, an attorney who filed his suit in 1969 against the city—the suit argued that city workers should not be forced to do political work. A federal judge ruled in Shakman's favor and the city agreed to abide by the decree. In July 1983, lawyers for Shakman and the city also agreed that political considerations were prohibited in hiring most of the city's 42,000 workers.[22] Some in the African American community were disappointed that Mayor Washington signed the Shakman court decree. They wanted those top-paying, good jobs—in over thirty major city departments—that had been denied to them for decades. Washington, however, intended to live up to the reform ideas of his mayoral campaign.

Past mayors disregarded the court decree. Instead of having control of over 42,000 city jobs—to use as patronage—like previous machine mayors, Washington only controlled about nine hundred top-level administrative jobs that were Shakman-exempt. In the jobs he did control Washington tried to be fair in his hiring practices. He hired African Americans, White people, women, and some Puerto Ricans to top decision-making city jobs. For the first time in decades, there were Black and Brown faces at City Hall. He hired Benjamin

Reyes as his administrative assistant, Maria Cerda to head the Mayor's Office of Employment and Training, and Gini Sorrentini to head the city's graphics department. About 40 percent of his top appointments were women.[23]

A small group of Mexican community leaders met privately with the mayor and expressed disappointment that he was hiring mostly Puerto Ricans, and very few Mexicans to his administration. Mayor Washington quickly learned that Latino groups use the term "Latino" mainly as a show of force, and for political mobilization purposes. Yet each specific Latino group expected political spoils and jobs. Mayor Washington subsequently appointed Jesús García and Juan Velázquez to top, high-paying positions as deputy commissioners in the city's departments of Water and Streets and Sanitation.[24] He appointed the popular Mexican family doctor, Jorge Prieto, as president of the Chicago Board of Health. Washington's record on Latino hires, compared to other mayors, indeed looked good. According to writer Gary Rivlin, "Dollars to Latino contractors increased tenfold between 1982 and 1985. The Washington administration was hiring Latinos at a high rate (eleven percent in 1985) than Byrne's (seven percent). Twenty-seven Latinos served in what could be called decision-making positions; under Byrne there were only three. Twenty percent of all Washington's appointments to the city boards and commissions were Latino."[25]

Washington was accused by his political opponents and some in the media of acting like an old-fashioned political "boss" and using city jobs, affirmative action, women and minority business "set aside" programs, and open bidding on city contracts to reward his friends. Washington stated that patronage was dead, but he insisted those programs were necessary to help the groups that had been excluded from the benefits of city government for so long. Washington was definitively not a boss like Mayor Richard J. Daley. However, Washington used executive orders and affirmative action programs in his first administration to reward his core constituency.[26]

Special Ward Elections

Washington encountered strong aldermanic opposition in the City Council for the first three years of his first term. In what became known as "Council Wars," Edward "Fast Eddie" Vrdolyak, the Tenth Ward alderman, lead a majority bloc of twenty-nine predominately White aldermen who opposed Washington at every turn. Washington had twenty-one aldermen who backed

him. The "Vrdolyak 29" thwarted Washington by blocking his appointments
to boards and commissions and his proposed policy initiatives. For decades
the City Council was a docile, rubber-stamp body that rarely opposed the
policies of previous mayors. But with Washington, the Vrdolyak 29 suddenly
wanted to share power with the mayor. Unlike Mayor Jane M. Byrne, however,
Washington was not going to capitulate to the Vrdolyak 29.

Mayor Washington supported Mexican candidates like Jesús García and
Juan Soliz for political office. With the combined strength of Mexican and
Black votes, Latinos began to win political office. In 1984, about 71 percent of
the Twenty-Second Ward's African America voters backed García in his defeat of incumbent Frank Stemberk in the March 20 election for Democratic
committeeman. Soliz, a young Mexican attorney, was elected to the Illinois
State Legislature in 1984, from the Twentieth District, which encompasses
the Pilsen and Little Village area. The African American vote helped Soliz,
who won by only fifty-seven votes.[27] He became the first Mexican elected
to the Illinois House. The year 1986 was historic for Latinos who had struggled for decades to acquire a political voice. The federal court ordered that
special aldermanic elections take place on March 16, 1986, in four Latino and
three African American city wards. In the redrawn Thirty-First Ward, Miguel Santiago won with support from the regular Democratic Party. Mayor
Washington backed Jesús García for alderman of the newly redrawn Twenty-
Second Ward. Frank Stemberk declined to seek reelection. Instead party regulars slated a couple of Latino candidates to run against García, but ultimately
García won.

In the Twenty-Fifth Ward, State Representitive Juan Soliz decided to run
for alderman. Soliz first ran for representative as an independent, antima-
chine candidate. He once called the people working in Vito Marzullo's organization "thugs and goons." He also described Marzullo as an old man disconnected from the community.[28] Once a supporter of Mayor Washington,
Soliz denounced the mayor for supposedly dragging his feet on Latino hiring.
Soliz was supported in his aldermanic race by alderman Edward Vrdolyak,
who agreed to help pay for Soliz's campaign debt. Soliz beat the Washington-
backed Juan Velázquez and won as alderman. Retired Vito Marzullo "was
there at Soliz's side the night of his aldermanic victory. Soliz watched the returns at Marzullo's headquarters, where he described Marzullo as a 'fine man'
from whom he had a lot to learn. Soliz won with forty-five percent of the
Latino vote and seventy-four percent of the white vote against three Latino

foes."[29] In the City Council, Soliz was squarely on Vrdolyak's side and a solid anti-Washington vote.[30] Soliz's reputation of jumping from one political camp to another won him few friends. He was eventually defeated as alderman and faded from the political scene.

Control of the City Council depended on who would win in the Twenty-Sixth Ward, a mostly Puerto Rican ward on the city's Northwest Side. Vrdolyak and Washington threw all their troops and resources into trying to win this decisive aldermanic seat. Manuel Torres, a tall, muscular bodybuilder was backed by Vrdolyak, Byrne, and Daley. The diminutive Luis Gutiérrez was backed by Washington and some of his council allies. Gutiérrez previously drove a cab for a living. Later, Washington gave Gutiérrez a stable, well-paying city job as a deputy superintendent with the Department of Streets and Sanitation. Gutiérrez beat Torres among Latino voters and received the majority of the votes coming from the 11 percent of the ward that was African American; the White vote went overwhelmingly for Torres. The final results had Gutiérrez ahead of Torres by twenty votes. Since Gutiérrez won more than 50 percent of the votes, he obviously won the election. A couple of weeks later, however, Torres's lawyers announced that they had thirty-one affidavits signed by voters claiming to have written in Jim Blasinski's name as a write-in candidate.

The Board of Election Commissioners (BOEC) also claimed to have found nine more Blasinski votes, bringing his count to a perfect forty to force a runoff. The missing votes were supposedly discovered in ballot boxes left unsealed at the board's warehouse. After several weeks, the courts ordered that a runoff would need to be held. Gutiérrez's new buttons read "RE-ELECT GUTIERREZ."[31] Washington and Gutiérrez were convinced Vrdolyak and his political machine friends at the BOEC, were trying hard to steal the election. Both Torres and Gutiérrez engaged in mudslinging and character assassination. In October 1984, a Molotov cocktail was thrown through the front window of Gutiérrez's home. At the time, Gutiérrez was home with his family. For three months they lived in a hotel room. He blamed the attack on those who opposed reform and Mayor Washington.[32] The case was never solved.

Torres then made a serious tactical mistake—the day before the election he agreed to debate Gutiérrez on the Spanish-language television station, Channel 44. Gutiérrez had lived in Puerto Rico for several years and spoke fluent Spanish, while Torres spoke very little Spanish. During the debate Gutiérrez spoke in eloquent Spanish. Torres, however, struggled to put his sentences together. Then, as Gutiérrez recalled in his memoir, Torres said, "I'm going to speak in English for the rest of the debate. That is the language I will need to be alderman of the 26th Ward. Everyone deserves to understand what we say here tonight."[33] Many Latinos were insulted that Torres choose to speak English instead of Spanish. Torres's mistake probably cost him the election. Torres lost the runoff by just under a thousand votes. The division of seats as twenty-nine to twenty-one that had stopped Washington from effectively governing was reconfigured into a twenty-five to twenty-five draw, with Mayor Washington holding the tie-breaking vote. Washington finally gained control over the council and Council Wars ended.

A growing number of new and reform-minded African American and Latino leaders were elected to office, clinging to Washington's long coattails.[34] After the election, Juan Soliz called for unity among his fellow Latino aldermen, but they ignored him. Political writer David Fremon, noted, "There was so little unity that both Soliz and new 22nd Ward alderman Jesús García celebrated their inauguration by hiring different mariachi bands to serenade outside council chambers—surely the first Battle of the Mariachi Bands in city hall history."[35] Two *Chicago Tribune* reporters added, "Mariachi players with wailing trumpets and bass guitars swelled the hallways with Mexican ballads and folk songs. The visitors' gallery was packed with Latino voters, many of whom chanted 'Soliz,' and 'Chuy,' García's nickname, as the aldermen made their way through the chambers, representatives of a community with a new-found voice."[36]

Gutiérrez became the unofficial leader of the council's Latino aldermen, and a spokesman for Mayor Washington. Once, Washington was trying to pass a property tax hike but was getting strong opposition from Edward Vrdolyak. Washington called Luis Gutiérrez into his office and asked if he would read aloud, in the City Council, the private property tax bills of Vrdolyak and his allies to demonstrate that they regularly underpaid taxes on their homes. At the next City Council meeting, Gutiérrez began publicly announcing the property tax bills of the Vrdolyak bloc aldermen. The aldermen were deeply offended and Vrdolyak jumped to his feet and yelled at Gutiérrez. In his memoir, Gutiérrez recalled that Vrdolyak yelled, "This is my home. You have made a mistake. Are you so vile? So petty? So venal? I will never address you directly or indirectly on this council floor."[37] When Gutiérrez announced what First Ward alderman Fred Roti paid in taxes, Fiftieth Ward alderman Bernie Stone, Roti's best friend, stood up with his face red in anger, and started screaming at Gutiérrez, "I paid the taxes each and every year. I never asked anyone for a break. How dare you come in here, you little pipsqueak."[38]

There was a lot of yelling and chaos in the council and Mayor Washington quickly adjourned the meeting. The television reporters loved the drama and the contentious meeting was shown on every television channel that evening. The next day all the major newspapers had the word "pipsqueak" in their morning editions. Mayor Washington called Gutiérrez and said, "That was wonderful. I loved it. Those hypocrites. Thanks, Lou."[39]

In 1987, Raymond Figueroa, a Puerto Rican attorney, with Washington's backing, defeated Miguel Santiago to become alderman of the Thirty-First Ward. A year later Figueroa defeated Joseph Berrios for committeeman of the ward. Also in 1987, with Washington's backing, Miguel del Valle beat veteran Edward Nedza to become the first Latino state Senator in Illinois. Miguel del Valle was regarded as a progressive, independently minded legislator. "One important piece of legislation I introduced is the bilingual pay supplement," said del Valle. "The state pays a little more to employees who use a second language in their line of work. I also worked directly on creating judicial subcircuits in Cook County, which lead, for the first time, to the election of a number of Latinos to the bench. People like David Delgado and other Latinos have won positions as judges in the judicial circuit court system."[40]

Jesús García was also a progressive rising star of the growing Latino independent political movement. In 1986, he was elected alderman of the Twenty-Second Ward. He was reelected to the City Council in 1991. In 1992, he was elected to the Illinois Senate and reelected in 1996. García said, "I enacted legislation to improve health care and protect consumers from being ripped off by unscrupulous immigration practitioners called notaries, or notary publics, who pass themselves off as immigration specialists and lawyers."[41] United States Representative García firmly believes that political empowerment for Latinos began with Harold Washington. "It reiterates how progressive and visionary Harold Washington was. He opened the doors of government for Latinos," said García. "And even Latinos and Latinas who have been elected to Congress or to statewide positions like Controller of Illinois, or City Clerks like Miguel del Valle and Anna Valencia, if we had not had the opening of government, the way it took place in the eighties, some of these things might not have occurred. I may not be going to Congress. Luis Gutiérrez would not have gone to Congress if we had not fought for the Voting Rights Act and the lawsuits had not come about."[42]

Latino Commission

Under Mayor Washington, several new commissions were established to address the concerns of Latinos, Asian Americans, women, and gays and lesbians. On October 5, 1983, fifteen Latino community leaders who had campaigned for Washington announced in the press room of the second floor of City Hall that they were forming a Commission on Latino Affairs. Washington followed through on his campaign pledge to create the commission and, days later, signed an executive order creating the Mayor's Commission on Latino Affairs (MCLA). Writer Gary Rivlin noted, "But where he (Washington) envisioned a benign city agency that would collect statistics showing he was in every way the ideal mayor from the Latino perspective, his Latino allies had in mind an independent commission that would serve as the Latino community's advocate within the bureaucracy."[43]

María de los Angeles Torres was the director of the fifteen-member MCLA in 1983. Torres is now a college professor of political science who writes books on the Cuban experience. One controversial aspect of the Commission's work was a regular six-month report where they graded the mayor on Latino hiring and the awarding of city contracts to Latino businesses. The report was sent to the press. The report highlighted the lack of Latino employees in specific city departments and challenged the mayor and department heads to hire more Latinos. The Commission once gave Washington a "D" grade because not one of the new twenty-six managers that he named during his midterm shakeup was Latino.[44] The media had a field day with the Commission's reports, sensing cracks in the fragile African American, Latino, and White coalition that elected Washington.

Many African Americans felt that Latinos were ungrateful and pushy by publicly criticizing the mayor. African American Eighth Ward alderman "Marian Humes was always mouthing off during the caucus about how much the fat-cat Latinos were getting from this administration," Jesús García said. "We were getting too many jobs, too many contracts, too many appointments—all at the expense of her constituents. Marian would needle your ass."[45]

Torres genuinely liked Harold Washington, but as head of the MCLA, she felt compelled to demand that the city hire more Latinos. "I think Harold Washington tried to be fair in bringing in Whites, Blacks, and Latinos into City Hall," said Torres. "He had less resources than his predecessors. As mayor, he signed the Shakman decree that limited political hiring and firings. . . . When the mayor was accused of not being fair, he did take it person-ally."[46] Mayor Washington indeed did take it personally. He thought Latinos, "Were too pushy, aggressive beyond their readiness to compete. . . . They're mau-mauing us, and I'm getting tired of it," he complained.[47] Washington also became angry that Latinos publicly aired their grievances and arguments in-stead of keeping them "within the family."[48]

The critical hiring reports from the MCLA kept coming. Many top city administrators became irritated when the reports showed they lacked Latino employees in their departments. "But you know what the mayor told me about the perception that Latinos were being too pushy? That he would be doing the same thing," said Torres.[49] In September of 1987, Torres stepped down as the head of the MCLA. "I don't know of any mayor who would allow us to do what we did with the MCLA," said Torres. "Mayor Jane Byrne sort of opened the door of city government to Latinos. Yet Washington opened city govern-ment to Latinos and developed a more respectful relationship with Latinos. He helped Latinos get elected to political office and develop an independent style of Latino political power."[50]

Congressman Jesús García concurred, "Mayor Washington really opened up the doors of government in Chicago for communities that had been left out: Blacks, Latinos, women, gays and lesbians, and Arabs. One of his most lasting actions as it pertains to Latinos and immigrants is his executive order in 1985 barring any city collaboration with the immigration service. Harold is the father of sanctuary cities in America."[51] In addition to making Chicago a sanctuary city that protected immigrants, Mayor Washington—in a display of compassion—visited Mexico City in 1985 to offer aid to victims of a terrible earthquake. He also visited San Juan, Puerto Rico.

Improved Neighborhood Services

Mayor Washington pushed for economic development in African American and Latino neighborhoods and not just in the downtown area. Residents now had four Latino aldermen in office who would listen and act on their concerns. City services in their neighborhoods vastly improved. Jesús García recalled, "As alderman, residents came to me complaining about basic city services like garbage pickup, bait for rodents, street cleaning, abandoned cars, and street-lights."[52] Many city streets in Latino neighborhoods were newly paved and new sidewalks were installed or repaired. Washington practiced an open style of government and annually held public hearings in neighborhoods across the city so residents could have input on policy making and how the city's yearly budget should be allocated. Upon entering office, Washington inherited a huge financial deficit in the city budget, but he managed to balance the budget. Under Washington, the major downtown credit agencies restored the city's bond rating to the "A" level.

Scandal

The Washington administration was not scandal free. In early 1986, a federal investigation, "Operation Incubator," had wired an informer, Michael Raymond, who recorded a few pro-Washington aldermen and city employees soliciting bribes. The mayor was forced to fire John Adams, second in command in the city's revenue department, for illegally accepting an alleged payoff of ten thousand dollars. Washington also suspended the head of that scandal-ridden department.[53] One month later, Clarence McClain, Washington's close friend and considered to be the new mayor's "patronage chief," was back in the news. Clarence McClain had a bad reputation due to a string of vice convictions which included pimping and keeping a house of prostitution. He had been forced out of the Washington administration after a public outcry in 1983.[54] The "Operation Incubator" investigation showed that McClain still had "clout" at City Hall and had stopped the awarding of a multimillion-dollar collections contract. Washington was forced to disown his old friend.[55] Some political pundits wondered why there was very little public moral outrage about "Operation Incubator" from reformers and liberals, who had been critical of corruption in the Daley administration. Former Alderman Leon Despres, when interviewed, "Dismissed any comparison, saying that corruption under Washington was 'petty' and not systematic as it was under Daley."[56]

1987 Mayoral Campaign

In the 1987 mayoral campaign, Washington selected as his running mates Cecil Partee, an African American, for city treasurer and Gloria Chevere, a Puerto Rican woman, for city clerk. Some African American community leaders denounced Washington's selection of Chevere, as they preferred that an African American individual run for city clerk. Some African American were convinced that Latinos could not win elected office by their own efforts and were again riding Washington's coattails. Tensions periodically flared up between African American and Latino supporters of Washington. One angry African American alderman argued that Latinos exaggerated their voting strength and collectively could not put together enough votes to even elect a dog catcher. Yet Washington realized the Latino vote was crucial if he hoped to win reelection. Washington figured that in 1987, as happened in 1983, the city's "swing vote" would be located along the independent lakefront wards and in Latino neighborhoods. Washington, as he did in 1983, once again engaged in effective coalition building. In the primary both Washington and challenger Jane M. Byrne spend considerable time and effort courting Latino voters. At numerous Latino stops, the charismatic Washington would deliver excellent, serious speeches about his desire to be a fair mayor and include previously marginalized groups like Latinos, in the active governance of the city. He would then switch his tone, flash his infectious smile, and use humor to win over his audience.

In the primary, Washington beat Jane M. Byrne. And in the general election he went on to beat his main challenger, Tenth Ward alderman Edward Vrdolyak. He beat Vrdolyak by almost 132,000 votes while winning close to 54 percent of the total three-way mayoral votes cast.[57] Once again, a large percentage of Latinos voted for Washington. Washington's general and primary vote totals showed that he made significant vote percentage improvement in the four Latino wards. In the Twenty-Fifth and Thirty-First Wards, his vote percentage increased by more than 10 percent, while in the Twenty-Second and Twenty-Sixth Wards, they increased by more than 6 percent.[58] Gloria Chevere did not win in her bid to become city clerk. Years later, she would become a Cook County Circuit judge.

Washington demonstrated during his first term that he was a very qualified, fair mayor who did a lot of good things for the city. Still, a lot of White people could not find it in their hearts to vote for an African American. He won his second term with about 17 percent of the White vote, a little more than the first time he won. Washington was disappointed. He repeatedly said that he wanted to be Chicago's mayor for the next twenty years. But on November 25, 1987, the day before Thanksgiving, Mayor Harold Washington died while still in office of a sudden heart attack.

Many Chicagoans, especially African American Chicagoans, were stunned and saddened. They viewed Washington as a hero. The mayor's body laid in state at City Hall where tens of thousands of people, including national politicians, filed by and paid their last respects. The city mourned for five days. Chicago's new Central Library, a junior college, a federal building, and five other parks and buildings, were named in honor of Harold Washington. Many were left to wonder what Washington, who finally had full control of the City Council, could have achieved had he lived longer. What would have been Washington's legacy had he served as the city's mayor for several more terms?

There is no doubt that political empowerment for Latinos began when they teamed up with Harold Washington. Washington actively campaigned in Puerto Rican and Mexican wards during his two campaigns for mayor. Latinos effectively engaged in coalition politics with African Americans and progressive White people to help Washington get elected as the city's first African American mayor in 1983 and then again in 1987. In return, Washington helped Latinos in numerous ways. He hired a good number of Latinos to high-paying, top decision-making city jobs in his administration. Before Washington, there were few Latinos employed at City Hall. But Washington opened up city government for Latinos. He also appointed Latinos to important city boards and commissions.

Washington established the MCLA, which gave Latinos a strong voice at City Hall. The relationship between the MCLA and the mayor was not always friendly, and the MCLA consistently advocated that Mayor Washington and the heads of major city departments hire even more Latinos. City contracts to Latino businesses also improved significantly under the Washington administration.

Washington supported and campaigned for various Latinos who ran for elected office such as Luis Gutiérrez, Jesús García, Raymond Figueroa, and Miguel del Valle. With Washington's support, combined with African American and Latino votes, these individuals were able to win city and statewide offices for the very first time. Washington encouraged an independent, progressive style of Latino political power. And once in office, these Latino elected officials pushed for better city services in Latino neighborhoods.

SOCIALIST CANDIDATE

FOR ALDERMAN 15TH WARD

WM. E. RODRIGUEZ

William Emilio Rodríguez, Socialist candidate for alderman of the 15th Ward, featured in the Socialist newsletter of 1914. He was the first Spanish-speaking person elected to Chicago's City Council in 1915. Courtesy Chicago History Museum, ICHi-092960-003-01; *Chicago Sun-Times* photographer.

William Emilio Rodríguez, alderman of the 15th Ward, sitting in a courtroom, Chicago, Illinois, February 24, 1916. Rodríguez defended Mrs. Waller Page Easton, a victim of "Big Bill" Thompson's shakedown of city employees. Courtesy Chicago History Museum, DN-0065904, *Chicago Daily News* negatives collection.

A musical group playing traditional Puerto Rican Christmas music, serenade the Mayor and Mrs. Daley outside their home on January 6, 1964. Jan. 6 is Three Kings Day celebrated by the city's Puerto Rican community. Courtesy Chicago History Museum, ICHi-092960; *Chicago Sun-Times* photographer.

Special tribute to Richard J. Daley in City Hall chambers, marking the 10th anniversary of his death, December 26, 1986. Seated left, Richard M. Daley, standing, Mayor Harold Washington, seated right, Abraham Lincoln Marovitz. Courtesy Chicago History Museum, ICHi-022462.

Richard J. Daley dons a Mexican sombrero for the Holiday Folk Fair in 1973 at Navy Pier. Photo: Laszlo Kondor. RJD_04_01_0029 _0005_013. Richard J. Daley collection, University of Illinois Chicago Library.

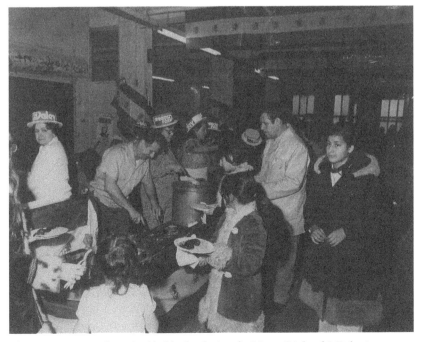

The group 'Amigos for Daley,' hold a fundraiser for Mayor Richard J. Daley in 1975. Courtesy Richard J. Daley Collection, University of Illinois at Chicago Library.

Left to right, Adeline Keane, unidentified actor, Mayor Richard J. Daley, actor Frank Lovejoy, Eleanor Daley, and Thomas Keane at The Best Man" theater event in 1961. Leonard Bass, Quality Photographers, Inc. RJD_04_01_0020_0004_001. Richard J. Daley collection, University of Illinois Chicago Library.

Eleventh Ward Alderman Michael Bilandic at the podium during a campaign event for Mayor Richard J. Daley in the early 1970s. Richard M. Daley is seated to the left. Chicago Fire Department. RJD_04_01_0029_0001_005. Richard J. Daley collection, University of Illinois Chicago Library.

Right to left, Mayor Richard J. Daley, Congressman Frank Annunzio, and Alderman Vito Marzullo, 25th Ward, in the reviewing stand of a downtown parade in the early 1970s. Copelin Commercial Photographers. JPCC_02_0001_0009_0016_0038. James Parker collection, University of Illinois Chicago Library.

Mayor Michael Bilandic. Courtesy, the Harold Washington Library Center, Municipal Reference Library.

Rudy Lozano, *right*, and attorney Juan Soliz, sporting blue Harold Washington campaign buttons in 1983. Courtesy Rudy Lozano Papers, University of Illinois at Chicago Library.

Harold Washington with Latino leaders at the Midland Hotel, 1983. (Left to right) Unidentified, Rudy Lozano, unidentified, Juan Soliz, Ray Castro, and Rev. Jorge Morales. Courtesy, Rudy Lozano Papers, University of Illinois at Chicago Library.

Latinos hold up "Latinos for Washington" signs at a political rally in 1983 at the University of Illinois at Chicago, two weeks before the mayoral primary. Over 12,000 supporters attended the rally, which became a turning point in Washington's campaign. Courtesy Rudy Lozano Papers, University of Illinois at Chicago Library.

A large crowd attends the funeral of Rudy Lozano in June 1983. The crowd walked through the streets of Pilsen and Little Village. Courtesy Rudy Lozano Papers, University of Illinois at Chicago Library.

Mayor Jane M. Byrne
and her daughter
Kathy, *left*, hold Puerto
Rican flags in the
reviewing stand of the
Puerto Rican parade
in downtown Chicago
in 1979. Standing next
to the mayor are Jose
Perez and Juan Cruz,
officials of the Puerto
Rican Parade Commit-
tee. Courtesy Tomas V.
Sanabria.

Mayor Jane M. Byrne. Cour-
tesy Harold Washington Library
Center, Municipal Reference
Library.

Mayor Harold Washington at a campaign stop for Raymond Figueroa, running for 31st Ward alderman in 1987. *Left to right*, Miguel del Valle, Luiz Gutiérrez, Harold Washington, Raymond Figueroa, and Gloria Chevere. Courtesy Carlos Hernandez, Puerto Rican Arts Alliance.

Mayor Harold Washington shaking hands with young Latinos in a Mexican neighborhood in September 1985. Jesús García is to the right of the mayor. Courtesy Chicago Public Library, Special Collections, HWAC.

Mayor Richard M. Daley, Alderman Billy Ocasio 26th Ward (with hat), and U.S. Congressman Luis Gutiérrez (D-Ill) inaugurate Paseo Boricua a commercial strip on Division Street. The January 6, 1995 inauguration included the installation of two large, steel Puerto Rican flags on Western and California Avenues. Courtesy *La Raza*.

A large crowd attended in inauguration of Paseo Boricua on January 6, 1995. Courtesy Carlos Hernandez, Puerto Rican Arts Alliance.

CHAPTER FOUR

Eugene Sawyer and Richard M. Daley—A New Day?

Eugene Sawyer

After Mayor Harold Washington's death, even before he was buried, City Council aldermen were secretly meeting and bargaining to see who could come up with the necessary votes to be declared the next mayor of Chicago. Thirty-Third Ward alderman Richard F. Mell, a loyal member of the 29 aldermen who opposed Washington during the Council War years, desperately desired to become the new mayor. He worked the telephones feverishly trying to make deals with other aldermen for their vote. But Mell could not round up the necessary votes. Many Washington supporters, including the Latino aldermen, backed Fourth Ward alderman Timothy Evans, an African American man who had served as Washington's floor leader in the City Council. Many believed Evans was the heir apparent to Washington. Evans, as acting mayor, would supposedly continue pushing Washington's reform agenda. Many of the aldermen in the old anti-Washington bloc preferred Sixth Ward alderman Eugene Sawyer. These aldermen believed Sawyer, an African American man, could be controlled and then easily defeated in a special election.[1]

Sawyer was shy, pleasant, and nonconfrontational. In fact, Sawyer was so soft-spoken he was sometimes difficult to understand. Sawyer acknowledged he was often misunderstood. "I guess my quiet demeanor has sort of bothered you guys, and I hear you call me 'Mumbles,'" Sawyer said to reporters. "I do have a quiet demeanor, but that doesn't mean we don't move aggressively and get things done or that we don't have a handle on things. We do."[2] Fourteenth Ward alderman Edward Burke pushed hard to get the reluctant Eugene Sawyer to accept the position of acting mayor. At one point, Burke was yelling at Sawyer to accept the position. Monroe Anderson, former press secretary to Sawyer stated, "Sawyer could not overcome the image of the meek, weak, plantation-raised pol being ordered around by Burke, the zealous, vitriolic lieutenant of the anti-Washington council war."[3]

About four thousand demonstrators marched around City Hall on the night of the council election. They were backing the election of alderman Timothy Evans and they were accusing Sawyer of "selling out" to White politicians. The demonstrators yelled, "traitor," "no deals," and "Uncle Tom."[4] Alderman Edward Burke and the White aldermen who backed Sawyer, had high hopes that Sawyer would be a temporary, docile mayor, who would drive a deep wedge among the African American electorate. Finally, after all the secret deals were complete, a final vote was taken. Sawyer was named acting mayor with twenty-nine votes. "Sawyer was sworn in as mayor at four o'clock in the morning, 'like a thief in the night,' to borrow a phrase from Washington," recalled Monroe Anderson. "Hundreds of thousands of viewer-voters were still watching the live broadcasts, and many were turned off by what they saw."[5] Sawyer was immediately viewed unfavorably in the African American community. Only about 10 percent of the African American community favored Sawyer for acting mayor while two-thirds preferred Evans.[6]

Conflict with Latinos

As acting mayor, Sawyer stated that he would continue most of Washington's reform programs, and he retained most of Washington's reform cabinet; there were no mass firings at City Hall. To please Latinos, Sawyer also signed an executive order to continue the Mayor's Commission on Latino Affairs (MCLA). Relations between the new mayor and Latinos seemed to be going smoothly. But the peace did not last long. In January 1988, three Latino aldermen strongly criticized Mayor Sawyer for firing Maria Cerda as director of the Mayor's Office of Employment and Training. Cerda, a Puerto Rican woman, was one of Washington's first cabinet appointees. Cerda was replaced by Arturo Vázquez, a Mexican man, who was deputy commissioner in the city's Department of Economic Development. "The manner in which it was done was not very classy. Mayor Washington used to boast about the work of the office of employment and training," said then alderman Jesús García.[7] The Latino aldermen vowed to oppose Sawyer in the 1989 special elections. Monroe Anderson disagreed that Sawyer was attempting to split the Latino community. He said that Cerda had to be fired because she had expressed reservations in her ability to support Mayor Sawyer and his agenda.[8]

A year later, another misunderstanding occurred between Mayor Sawyer and Latinos. The mayor attended a Latino restaurant in the Loop and gladly accepted the endorsement of Twenty-Fifth Ward alderman Juan Soliz. There, he signed a piece of paper identified as the "Hispanic agenda." The Hispanic agenda said that Sawyer agreed to name Hispanics as superintendent of police and as heads of nine other major city departments.[9] Sawyer denied even signing such a document and never heard of such an agenda. Nevertheless, Sawyer committed himself to hire Latinos for 20 percent of city jobs without promises of what specific cabinet posts they would be.[10]

A report by the MCLA criticized Mayor Sawyer regarding the low number of Latinos hired in major city departments. The report underscored that 30 percent of patients using city health clinics were Latino, but the Chicago Department of Health had no Latinos in decision-making positions.[11] The report criticized the mayor for not addressing health issues in Latino communities like prenatal care, infant mortality, and AIDS. It also pointed out that the 7.2 percent hiring rate of Latinos in 1988 was the worst since the Byrne administration.[12] Mayoral spokesman Joel Werth expressed the administration's belief that MCLA was playing politics with their publicized health report, and they were not really pro-Sawyer people.[13]

Richard M. Daley, "Son of Boss"

Eugene Sawyer was an accidental mayor, who served less than two years in office. The Illinois Supreme Court ordered a special mayoral election for February 1989. Daley and his advisers had been meticulously planning for this moment; they recognized clearly that the ethnic and racial makeup of Chicago had drastically changed. Taking a note out of Washington's playbook, Daley had been engaging in coalition politics and reaching out to African American, White ethnics, and, especially, Latino voters. Many believed the fragile coalition between African Americans and Latinos formed during the Washington administration would hold together and elect Evans as mayor. However, the coalition splintered. In a surprise move, Twenty-Sixth Ward alderman Luis Gutiérrez endorsed Daley for mayor. Some Latinos and African Americans called Gutiérrez a traitor. They reminded him that it was Harold Washington and African American voters who got him elected. They felt he should have supported Evans. Gutiérrez defended himself by pointing to the polls, which showed that Daley was a sure winner with solid support from Puerto Ricans and White people.[14] Yet many wondered what Daley offered Gutiérrez for his support.[15]

Daley put together a coalition of White ethnics, lakefront residents, and Latinos. He defeated Eugene Sawyer in the primary 56 percent to 44 percent and Tim Evans in the general election 55 percent to 41 percent; Edward Vrdolyak received 4 percent of the vote.[16] In the primary, Daley received 71 percent of the Latino vote compared to 29 percent for Sawyer.[17] In the general election, Daley won 73 percent of the Mexican American vote and 78 percent of the Puerto Rican vote.[18] Writer Paul M. Green said that "Daley unleashed a massive display of political power as he began his march to the fifth floor of city hall [the mayor's office]. With almost military precision, Daley and his allies rolled over old foes, won over new allies, and demonstrated a surprising amount of tactical and strategic political shrewdness."[19]

Many voters and the media were obviously delighted that Richard M. Daley was elected mayor. Chicagoans were tired of the political and racial bickering that had taken place in the city over the last ten years. Daley was seen as a breath of fresh air, as a healing figure who would unite the city. The city's major newspapers and media outlets gave the new mayor glowing reviews and an extended honeymoon. It seemed like he could do no wrong. But a few seasoned reporters wondered if Daley would become a reform mayor like Washington, or an old-time boss like his father. Some in the media dubbed Daley as the "Son of Boss." But Daley insisted he was not going to be a machine-style boss like his father. In the public he worked hard to cultivate the image of a knowledgeable public servant who was working hard and looking out for the welfare of Chicago and its citizens.[20]

A Latino Congressman

Some of former alderman Luis Gutiérrez's supporters nicknamed him, "El Gallito," the little fighting rooster. He was a good orator in both English and Spanish and also a relentless campaigner.[21] In the City Council, Gutiérrez became one of Mayor Daley's closest Latino allies. For his loyalty, he was awarded the chairmanship of the Committee on Housing, Land Acquisition, Disposition and Leases, which controls and leases city-owned land. Daley also named Gutiérrez council president pro tempore, a ceremonial position where he chairs meetings in the mayor's absence.[22] In 1990, reapportionment created the state's first predominately Latino congressional district in Illinois.

The Latino district was drawn by federal court order to remedy past discrimination. In 1993, with Mayor Daley's endorsement, Luis Gutiérrez was elected as United States Congressman of that Fourth District. It was a historic victory for the Latino community as Gutiérrez became the first Latino congressman from Chicago. Daley backed Gutiérrez, many assumed, as a reward for his endorsement in the 1989 mayoral race.

Gutiérrez's district was an oddly shaped area linking the Mexican community on the Southwest Side, with the largely Puerto Rican community on the Near Northwest Side. Some nicknamed the C-shaped district "earmuffs" because of its peculiar shape. Opponents of the district, including a few conservative White people and Latinos, filed a lawsuit against the creation of the district saying it was a deliberate example of racial gerrymandering. They argued that the two Latino communities should not be lumped together because they are culturally different. Other Latino elected officials, and the Mexican American Legal Defense and Educational Fund, fought to protect the Fourth District boundaries. A federal court panel upheld the constitutionality of the district. Rep. Luis Gutiérrez (D-IL.) maintained staff offices in both the Mexican and Puerto Rican communities of Chicago. In Congress, he consistently sponsored legislation protecting the rights of undocumented workers, legal residents, and immigrants. He was well-liked among Mexicans in Chicago and appeared regularly on Spanish-language radio and television.

Gutiérrez was involved in controversy in 1998 over his failure to pay the right amount of property taxes on his expensive home in the gentrified neighborhood of Bucktown. While his neighbors paid over $5,000 yearly in property taxes, Gutiérrez paid just $275 on his property which was listed as a vacant lot by the Cook County assessor's office. After the story broke in the media, Gutiérrez quickly paid $7,500 in back taxes.[23] Ironically, Gutiérrez had once publicly accused machine politicians in the City Council of not paying their fair share of property taxes, and now he was caught in the same situation. Gutiérrez was reelected numerous times and served as congressman from 1993 to 2019, when he retired.

Latino Hiring and Political Empowerment

Mayor Daley pledged to honor the Shakman court decree prohibiting political hiring and firing. Soon after his election, the new mayor introduced a "rainbow" cabinet; half of the twenty-four appointees were minorities—African

American, Latino, and Asian.[24] Daley seemed willing to be fair in city hiring and to have an open government in the style of former Mayor Harold Washington. He even agreed to continue Washington's programs to assist minority- and women-owned businesses in receiving a fair share of city contracts. Daley said, "I think [Washington] would be very happy with my policies today, with my appointments and the committee we put together to protect the set-aside program"—a program which guides a share of city contracts to firms owned by minorities and women. "We're going to make the set-aside program work for all minority contractors in the city."[25]

In 1989, Daley appointed Miriam Santos, a Puerto Rican woman and a member of Daley's transition team, as City Treasurer. Santos succeeded Cecil Partee, who was appointed to Daley's old post of Cook County State's Attorney. In the 1990s, Daley appointed Latinos to top-level cabinet positions at City Hall. His appointments represented the major Latino groups in the city. Daley selected four Latinos to his cabinet, two were Mexican, one was Cuban, and another was Puerto Rican. The two Mexicans were Raymond Orozco as fire commissioner, and Mary Gonzales Koenig to head the Mayor's Office of Employment and Training. He appointed Reverend Daniel Alvarez, Cuban, to head the Department of Human Services. He appointed Ben Reyes, Puerto Rican, to head the department of General Services Administration.

Latinos were pleased with the hires. However, there was still an underrepresentation of Latinos at City Hall. As of April 1989, "Only 6.6 percent of the city's 41,108 employees were Hispanic," said Juan Molina, a researcher with the Chicago Commission on Latino Affairs. "About 14 percent of Chicago's work force is Hispanic."[26] One of Daley's top Latino appointments turned out to be an embarrassment. In 1992, Daley appointed longtime Chicago police officer Matt L. Rodriguez as superintendent of the 12,500 member Chicago Police Department (CPD). Rodriquez, who was Polish and Mexican became the first Latino to ever head the CPD. "Matt Rodriguez has the skills, knowledge and experience needed to elevate the Chicago Police Department to a new level of efficiency and effectiveness," Daley said.[27]

During his five-and-a-half years as superintendent, Rodriguez professionalized the department and promoted innovative programs like community policing. In 1997, however, the *Chicago Tribune* revealed that Matt Rodriguez was a close friend of Frank Milito, a convicted felon. Milito had been questioned in an unsolved murder case of the Amoco oil company executive Robert Merriam. The Chicago Police Department prohibits police officers from fraternizing with convicted felons.[28] The next day, Rodriguez retired from the police department and said, "The disclosure of his thirty-year relationship with Milito had 'pained' Mayor Richard M. Daley."[29] Milito was North Side businessman who owned several Amoco gas stations, a popular Italian restaurant, two travel agencies, and expensive real estate. Milito had taken Rodriguez on trips to Italy and Israel.[30]

Billy Ocasio, former alderman of the Twenty-Sixth Ward, believed Mayor Daley was very good for Latinos. "He has hired more Latinos than any other mayor," said Ocasio. "And he has given Latinos more city contracts than at any other time in the history of Chicago. Many of us worked for Harold Washington, but it was hard getting jobs. I know with this mayor, Latinos have gotten a lot more."[31] Luis Gutiérrez asked Mayor Daley to place Ocasio as Twenty-Sixth Ward alderman when he became Congressman. Daley agreed and Ocasio became alderman in January 1993. He explained that having Latino political representation is beneficial for Latino residents. "Having people like Miguel del Valle win a senate seat and Luis Gutiérrez win a congressional seat brings pride to Latinos," said Ocasio. "Politicians bring in more money and business development. . . . Some accomplishments in my ward include building the Humboldt Park Vocation Center and the Humboldt Park Library. We built the Ames Middle School. We built Paseo Boricua and did a lot of infrastructure repairs on Division Street."[32] In 1993, Daley appointed Ricardo Muñoz as alderman of the Twenty-Second Ward, and in 1996, he chose Daniel "Danny" Solis as alderman of the Twenty-Fifth Ward. Solis became one of the staunchest supporters of the mayor and his agenda.[33]

Feuds and Disagreements

As the number of appointed and elected Latino politicians grew, their differing political views often clashed. The debate over the future political status of the island of Puerto Rico, combined with politics at the neighborhood level, divided some Puerto Rican politicians. There was an ongoing feud between various Puerto Rican politicians and their allies during the late 1990s. One camp contained businessman and longtime, powerful former alderman Richard F. Mell of the Thirty-Third Ward and his allies, former Illinois state representative from the Fourth District Edgar López (D-Chicago) and former Alderman Vilma Colom of the Thirty-Fifth Ward. In the opposing camp were former Congressman Gutiérrez, former Twenty-Sixth Ward alderman

Billy Ocasio, and former state senator Miguel del Valle. Besides political differences, the two camps were fighting for control over local political power.
Gutiérrez and Ocasio publicly supported the independence of Puerto Rico
from the United States. Edgar López disliked the politics of Gutiérrez, Ocasio, and del Valle. "I understand the whole Puerto Rican independence movement. I even came out and publicly supported the release of what they call the
'political prisoners of war,' which I claim they're terrorists," said López. "I'm
for statehood for Puerto Rico."[34]

Edgar López is Puerto Rican and Ecuadorian. Some Puerto Ricans viewed
López as a loyal member of the Democratic machine. "There is no difference
between them and us," said López. "I don't take orders from anybody. Who
put Luis Gutiérrez there? Who keeps Billy Ocasio there? Mayor Richard M.
Daley put them there. Gutiérrez and Ocasio call themselves independent. The
only thing they did is put some Puerto Rican flags and some brick seats on
Division Street."[35] The bickering between the two sides got downright dirty.
An anonymous, crude newspaper called El Pito (the Whistle) was widely cir-
culated in Humboldt Park. It made wild accusations against Gutiérrez, Ocasio,
and del Valle. It poked fun at their politics and sexuality and accused them of
being women, gay, and bisexual. It also portrayed them as fanatical supporters
of Puerto Rican independence in an effort to hurt their reelection chances.
"They think I'm the one doing El Pito," said López. "Well, I don't do El Pito."[36]

López gained notoriety as chairman of a controversial 1998 state investigation into the alleged misuse of $150,000 of state education funds for low-
income students at Roberto Clemente High School in Humboldt Park. The
investigation alleged that instead of buying books, pencils, and school sup-
plies the local school council spent the money on a campaign to promote
Puerto Rican independence. No one was charged with wrongdoing.[37] López
was elected to the Illinois House in 1993. He was a four-term state representative and he envisioned a bright future for himself. "I would one day like to
be Speaker of the House. Maybe someday become governor of the state," said
López.[38]

But in the March 2000 primary, López faced a tough challenge from Cynthia Soto, a young Mexican woman. López received heavy support from Illinois's Republican governor George H. Ryan, Mayor Richard M. Daley, and
Joseph Berrios, commissioner of the Cook County Board of Review. Gutiérrez, Ocasio, and del Valle poured plenty of money and troops into Soto's campaign. Surprisingly, Soto scored a huge upset and defeated López. She went

on to serve in the Illinois House of Representatives from 2001 to 2019. After Soto's victory, Puerto Rican politicians held a news conference to announce a new, independent political coalition between Puerto Ricans and Mexicans. However, only about eighty people, mostly Puerto Ricans showed up at the conference. It appeared a lot of effort was still needed to bring Puerto Ricans and Mexicans into a lasting political coalition. One major problem that the two groups faced in establishing a strong coalition was that Mexicans and Puerto Ricans lived in different sections of the city, far away from each other. Through the years, the two groups have not reached out to each other in their quest for political empowerment.

Demise of the MCLA

During his first term in office, Mayor Daley stated that he would practice an inclusive, open-government style of management. He said that he would give his commissioners a free hand in running their departments. It soon became clear, however, that the mayor called the shots at City Hall, and he relied on a small inner circle of about four aides to carry out his agenda. Daley was not about to let the MCLA publicly criticize him and his record on hiring Latinos like they had under Mayors Washington and Sawyer. Daley stripped the ethnic advisory commissions of much of their influence.[39] Daley put the different commissions—women, veterans, Latinos, gays and lesbians, and Asian people—under the Human Relations Commission. The once active and vocal commissions became silent. "Mayor Daley hates to be criticized. He's very autocratic," said María de los Angeles Torres. "He comes into office and places the MCLA under the city's Human Relations Commission, where it's basically a do-nothing commission."[40]

Education Mayor

Mayor Daley was praised for his willingness to tackle the problem of poor education. Many city schools were overcrowded and falling apart from years of deferred maintenance. In late 1987, US Secretary of Education William J. Bennett came to Chicago to attend an education forum and he called Chicago schools the "worst in the nation."[41] Daley was dubbed the "education mayor" by the media. In 1989, Daley selected Lourdes Monteagudo, a Cuban woman, as the city's first deputy mayor of education. Monteagudo's role was to champion public education. Yet her daughter attended a private school in the affluent suburb of Winnetka. A reporter asked her why and Monteagudo allegedly said that "No Chicago public school is good enough for my daughter."[42] She later denied saying it. But the controversy pressured the mayor to fire her. Daley did not appoint anyone else to the post of deputy mayor of education.

On April 2, 1991, Daley was reelected to a four-year term with 70.7 percent of the vote over R. Eugene Pincham an African American. Daley was very popular in the White ethnic wards and Latino wards, and his popularity kept growing among African American voters. In 1995, Mayor Daley persuaded the Illinois Legislature to give him more direct control of the city's school system. The mayor appointed a five-member School Reform Board of Trustees which had wide powers to implement school policy. He placed his top aides, Paul Vallas and Gery Chico, as chief executive officer of the schools and as president of the board, respectively. Chico was Daley's former chief of staff. Vallas is White and Chico's father is Mexican and his mother is Greek and Lithuanian. "We have a long list of accomplishments," said former board president Gery Chico. "One, we established a sound financial footing for the school system. Two, we established eight years of labor peace with the teachers. Three, we've put in place a core curriculum and a sound education plan, which have led to three years of rising test scores. Four, we have the most aggressive capital improvement program of any place in the United States. We made $2 billion available in the renovation and building of new schools in Chicago."[43]

Gery Chico walked a thin ethical line by being school board president while lobbying for private companies. The law firm he worked with, Altheimer and Gray, was a City Hall lobbyist. Yet neither Mayor Daley nor Chico saw any conflict of interest with his role as a lobbyist. Years later, however, Paul Vallas criticized Chico's lobbying while serving as board president. "Chico's law firm received over $500 million in contracts from the school board during his tenure. As a lobbyist for the now-defunct law firm of Altheimer and Gray during his tenure as board president, Chico abstained from over 500 votes that affected his clients," Paul Vallas said.[44] From 1995 to 2001, school officials built twenty-seven new schools, twenty-four additions, twenty-seven annexes, and more than one hundred modular classrooms. "President Clinton and I toured one of our new schools. He thought it was the best thing since sliced bread. The kids were so happy to be in a new school," said Chico.[45] Despite the improvements, the Mexican American Legal Defense and Educational Fund reported that of 453 Chicago public elementary schools, 149 were overcrowded and 71 severely overcrowded schools were majority Latino.[46]

Additional new schools were a welcome sight to Latino and African American parents and students. Yet some questioned whether the city was taking on too much debt and risking the future fiscal stability of the schools and the city. Civic groups were urging Mayor Daley and school officials to lobby state and federal government for more education dollars. And even with an additional $1 billion, Chicago schools still needed about $2 billion more to meet the challenges of overcrowded schools, rising enrollments, and aging facilities.[47] Gery Chico and Paul Vallas pushed for the construction of two selective high schools to cater to gifted students: Walton Payton and North Side Prep. These schools cost over $40 million apiece. The two schools are among Illinois's most highly acclaimed selective-enrollment high schools. A political reporter noted, "North Side Prep came to be known as 'Chico High' because it was built in time for Chico's daughters to attend."[48]

Mexican parents were promised that a third new high school would be built to relieve overcrowding in the Little Village neighborhood. But school officials later admitted they did not have funds. A handful of Mexican mothers in Little Village pitched tents in a large vacant lot and staged a highly publicized, two-week hunger strike to persuade school officials to build the new high school. The striking mothers scored a victory in 2001 when school officials declared that funds would be allocated for two new high schools, one in Pilsen and one in Little Village. Each school would cost over $30 million.[49] In 2001, both Gery Chico and Paul Vallas left the school system amid Mayor Daley's dissatisfaction with dropping test scores. But Chico was still Mayor Daley's go-to guy; Daley appointed him president of the Chicago Park District and president of the Chicago City Colleges.

Hired Trucks and Corruption

In January 2004, the *Chicago Sun-Times* published its "Clout on Wheels" investigation where they discovered that privately owned dump trucks and drivers were paid under no-bid contracts and often sat idle all day, doing no work. The forty-million-dollar yearly program involved payoffs, sweetheart deals, connections to organized crime, and ties to Daley's family and friends.[50] Some of the easy money went to politically connected individuals and to trucking companies in the Eleventh Ward who, during a ten-year period, gave $840,000 in campaign contributions to the mayor and other politicians.[51]

The *Chicago Sun-Times* reporters discovered that for seven years, the Hired Truck Program was run by Angelo Torres, a city employee.[52] Federal prosecutors arrested Angelo Torres and he was convicted and sentenced to two years in prison for shaking down trucking-firm owners for cash for Mayor Daley's political campaign. Mayor Daley said he did not know who hired Angelo Torres. At his sentencing hearing, Torres said, "I worked very hard in my life to get where I got, and I unfortunately abused my authority, and for that reason I am apologetic. . . . When money came to me, I accepted it."[53] Eventually, forty-six people were indicted in the Hired Truck scandal, and nearly all pleaded guilty or were convicted.

The Hired Truck scandal led the Federal Bureau of Investigation (FBI) to suspect that political corruption was prevalent in the Daley administration. An FBI investigation later uncovered widespread patterns of questionable hiring practices in City Hall. Robert Sorich, a longtime City Hall insider from Daley's Bridgeport neighborhood, was assistant director of the Mayor's Office of Intergovernmental Affairs (IGA) from 1993 to 2005, and Daley's longtime patronage chief. Sorich's father was Richard J. Daley's photographer. Federal prosecutions charged that Sorich rigged test results and faked personnel interviews to reward political workers with well-paying city jobs and promotions in violation of the Shakman court decree.

At the Sorich trial in 2006, two former city officials, Donald Tomczak and Joe Gagliano, admitted that they organized hundreds of city workers into groups to work in political campaigns, and then lobbied for jobs and promotions for their members.[54] After weeks of testimony, a judge sentenced Sorich to a forty-six-month prison term. At his sentencing Sorich said, "I tried to do my best, and I tried to be fair." US District Judge David Coar rejected that, saying Sorich sat near the top of a hiring system that amounted to corruption.[55] Two other former city officials, Timothy McCarthy and Patrick Slattery, and a former city worker, John Sullivan, were also convicted and sentenced in the rigged hiring scheme.

Daley defended his convicted city employees. He said, "I know all those young men personally, and their families, and they are very fine young men."[56] And Mayor Daley—just like his father did when scandals became public— always denied any knowledge of corruption in his administration. However, the *Chicago Sun-Times* stated, "The 2006 trial and conviction of Daley patronage chief Robert Sorich revealed that the generations-old Chicago tradition of patronage hiring had continued to thrive in secret since virtually the beginning of the mayor's reign."[57] Daley, with his attorney, were interviewed by the FBI about City Hall corruption, but the mayor was never charged with wrongdoing.

Hispanic Democratic Organization

When Daley was first running for mayor in 1989, he wanted Latinos on his side. Top Daley adviser Timothy Degnan, and Daley's brother William Daley met with a group of Latinos in the Southeast Side who once worked for Tenth Ward alderman Edward Vrdolyak. They broke from Vrdolyak when he became a Republican. The group was asked if they would be willing to help Daley get elected as mayor. The group agreed to work for Daley, and they called themselves the Hispanic Democratic Organization (HDO). Two of the main founders and leaders of HDO were Al Sanchez, a Tenth Ward precinct captain and Victor Reyes.

After Daley won his first election, Al Sanchez became the head of the city's Department of Streets and Sanitation, and Victor Reyes became Mayor Daley's political chief. It soon became clear that HDO was basically an old-fashioned political army formed with the mayor's blessing. The group, which some said should have been called the "Hispanic Daley Organization," was extremely loyal to the mayor and willing to do whatever he desired of them. In fact, Angelo Torres, who was convicted for running the corrupt Hired Truck Program was a top HDO member. HDO members donated funds, and actively worked in campaigns to reelect the mayor. *Chicago Tribune* reporters noted that "Though it has no official connection to the mayor, the Hispanic Organization is quickly transforming the city's political landscape. HDO has helped Daley snatch turf that was once an alderman's domain and wield control over the city's growing Hispanic community which has yet to coalesce as a political force."[58]

In return for their political work, HDO members expected to be rewarded with secure, high-paying city jobs and promotions. The HDO had an estimated one thousand members and was becoming a formidable, massive patronage army that raised money for the candidates that the mayor favored. They showed up on election day to work in campaigns and persuade voters to vote for the candidates the mayor was backing. Meanwhile, HDO leaders working at City Hall were doling out city jobs and promotions to HDO friends, relatives, and campaign workers.[59] It was estimated that in their heyday, over eight hundred HDO members received city jobs. HDO members were mostly employed in departments where HDO lieutenants held high-ranking posts. Daley had promised to obey the Shakman decree but it was clear that patronage hiring was alive and thriving. Michael Shakman, the Chicago attorney who successfully sued to end City Hall patronage under Daley's father, said that the HDO "sounds like a large-scale illegal patronage operation."[60]

Daley built what some political observers called a "new machine." He was accused of exercising autocratic authority to get what he wanted. Daley won the loyalty of aldermen in the City Council by allowing them to control city services and zoning in their wards. Also, by 1998, Daley had personally appointed twenty of the fifty City Council aldermen. He controlled a "rubber stamp" council—in the manner of his father's time—that automatically approved his policy initiatives without question.[61] The HDO supported candidates who Mayor Daley favored and punished those he disliked. The mayor had no use for politicians who were not subservient and loyal to him. For instance, Mayor Daley wanted his aide John Pope to become alderman in the heavily Latino Tenth Ward. So in 1999, the "HDO helped mayoral aide John Pope win the aldermen's seat in the 10th Ward on the far Southeast Side. The group supported Pope, who hadn't been active in the community, even though his opponents included four Hispanics."[62]

In the March 1998 primaries, the HDO channeled troops and funds to defeat Jesús García. The HDO backed Antonio "Tony" Muñoz, a Chicago cop. Muñoz was a no-name opponent with no legislative experience. Yet, in a stunning defeat, Muñoz beat García, the six-year incumbent state senator. García picked up a majority of Latino votes but failed to win necessary votes in several White precincts. García lost the election by 960 votes out of nearly 13,000 cast. "Mayor Daley's hit squad came after us big time," said García. "They came after us because we challenged the mayor on fairness, on empowerment versus bossism, on our right to speak. . . . We were against the tax increment financing district for Pilsen. We were against low-income residents being displaced by high-income, white professionals."[63] García admits he ran a weak campaign and was concentrating instead on helping Sonia Silva get reelected. "Our mistake was not recognizing that this fight was perhaps the most serious challenge I faced. We assumed people knew our record. We didn't mobilize all our volunteers. We lost it to the great number of patronage workers the mayor put out there. We were outspent. They were successful because we fell asleep," said García.[64]

Alderman Daniel Solis of the Twenty-Fifth Ward was close friends with HDO members, and they worked on his reelection campaigns. Solis believed Jesús García lost because he, and other liberal Latino politicians were out of touch with the "new values" of Latino residents. "They project to the broader community that Hispanics are a victim, a minority group. As a victim, they are entitled to specific entitlements, like the African American community," said Solis. "Gentrification, police brutality, and bilingual education are not the top issues of the Latino community. Latino leaders should be pushing for jobs, homes, and naturalization."[65] Solis was one of Mayor's Daley's closest allies. The mayor rewarded Solis by naming him the City Council's president pro tempore. Solis believed Mayor Daley was a good mayor who helped Latinos. "If you look at Mayor Daley's record, his Latino appointments to top city positions have been outstanding. If you look at Latino neighborhoods, they are all improving in terms of better housing, education, and investment, said Solis."[66]

The HDO also set their sights on trying to defeat Sonia Silva. In March 1996, Sonia Silva defeated Fernando Frias, to become the first Mexican woman elected to the Illinois Legislature. She was from the First District, which included Little Village and Back of the Yards. Silva previously worked for about fifteen years for Jesús García when he was an alderman and state senator. She lived in Little Village. Silva was considered a progressive legislator. She did not like being called a politician. "The word 'politician' conjures a negative image. I think of myself more as a legislator. Legislators, like me, do not get huge $30,000 donations from political action committees. We have to do a lot of working raising funds for reelection every two years. We have dances, receptions, and banquets. It's ongoing, all the time. I rely on a lot of volunteers," said Silva.[67]

Silva was hurt that the HDO helped defeat her mentor, Jesús García. She said, "They don't want people who are independent voices. Some of the mayor's lobbyists came to my office and said, 'we want you to vote on this and this.' I would listen. But if I did not think it was positive, I would not vote for it. They want you to toe the party line, even if it goes against the interests of the community."[68] In March 1998, the HDO came after Sonia Silva. The HDO, along with the regular Democratic Organization supported Susana

Mendoza, a young Mexican woman. Running for political office is not for the faint of heart. "Many of my campaign workers are housewives. HDO members were pushing them, and calling them bad names," said Silva. "HDO people would surround me and say, 'bitch, you're going to go down.'... It's disheartening. Many people in this community have fought for years to have a voice."[69] Someone broke all the windows of Silva's daughter's car and slashed the tires, three times, on her son's car.

Silva survived the March 1998 election by beating Susana Mendoza. But in the March 2000 primary, Susanna Mendoza and hundreds of HDO members challenged Silva again. This time, however, of almost 5,000 votes cast, Mendoza beat Silva with about 850 votes. Some HDO members were active or former gang members. "I thought HDO were a bunch of thugs, rough along the edges," said Ben Joravsky, a political reporter for the *Chicago Reader*. "And when I would go to meetings it just seemed like they were ready to start punching at any minute. They acted like thugs, like gangsters."[70] The HDO's influence diminished considerably as a lengthy federal investigation looked into the group's role in rigging city hiring to get their members jobs and promotions. The rise of the once powerful HDO finally came to a halt in July 2008, when the group filed paperwork closing its campaign committee. In its final report to state elections officials, HDO leaders explained that they spent every last penny in their account in April.[71]

Then in February 2011, Al Sanchez—cofounder and leader of HDO, and former commissioner of Streets and Sanitation—was sentenced to two and a half years in prison for his role in rigging the city's hiring system, capping a federal investigation inside City Hall. His codefendant, former Chicago police officer Aaron del Valle was convicted of perjury and was sentenced to twelve months and a day.[72] Prosecutors said Sanchez handed city jobs to its members to build HDO, a pro-Daley patronage army.[73] In court, Sanchez argued that he was simply doing his job and he wanted to "empower Latinos." Mayor Daley in a statement said, "I feel bad for Al Sanchez and his family today because I knew him to be a hard-working employee, committed to do his best to serve the people of Chicago."[74] Sanchez's family were convinced that Al Sanchez was a scapegoat for higher-ranking city players. Asked who Sanchez was taking the fall for, his mother, Mary Sanchez, replied, "The main guy is up there, at City Hall."[75] Daley repeated his standard lines whenever scandals broke out in his administration: "I don't know nothing, and I have done nothing wrong." Victor Reyes left City Hall a clout-heavy attorney and he became a well-connected city lobbyist.

An Old Boss?

Former state senator Miguel del Valle insisted that Mayor Richard M. Daley created a political machine that expected absolute loyalty from Latino politicians. "I was very disappointed when Mayor Daley's hit squad, the HDO, went after and defeated state senator Jesús García," said del Valle. "The reason Daley's hit squad does not like us is because we stand up. We are critical when there is a need to be critical. I don't consider myself one of the boys."[76] Despite their political differences, Miguel del Valle eventually developed a close working relationship with Mayor Daley. To the surprise of many, Mayor Daley named del Valle as the new city clerk of Chicago in 2006. Many assumed that, by selecting del Valle, the mayor was hoping to draw attention away from the scandals that plagued his administration during the previous two years. Plus, the mayor was hoping to gather Latino support for his reelection bid.

Former United States Representative Luis Gutiérrez also once accused Daley of being a boss because the mayor's people tried to tell him what candidate to support in a presidential election. "I'm very disillusioned with Mayor Daley. He's acting like an old boss. Like his father," said Gutiérrez. "Illinois Democrats elected to Congress are supposed to be able to think and speak for themselves, not be directed in their political thinking by a boss from Chicago."[77] Gutiérrez and Mayor Daley later made up and supported each other. They blamed their past disagreements on poor communication.[78]

Daley Steps Down

After a long reign of twenty-two years, Daley decided to step down as mayor in September 2010; he served until 2011. Just like his father, he left a mixed legacy. Many people concluded that Daley vastly improved and beautified the city, especially the downtown area. His many green initiatives included the creation of a rooftop garden atop City Hall, the planting of thousands of trees and flowers, and creating miles of bicycle lanes. He created a lakefront park where Meigs Field once stood, by having city employees tear up the airplane runway in the middle of the night. After years of planning, Daley constructed the popular $475 million, 24.5-acre Millennium Park, which was praised by design critics and has become a front-yard showcase for Chicago. His most positive legacy includes many projects of his lakefront program and his efforts to beautify the city and encourage arts and culture.[79]

Daley was also praised for the expansion of Chicago's O'Hare International Airport and for improving public education. During his administration, new schools were constructed and repaired. He built numerous branch libraries in neighborhoods. He installed decorative wrought-iron fences around schools, parks, and libraries. Daley is commended for alleviating the racial chasms that existed in the city during the 1980s and for bringing diverse Chicagoans together. He is credited with having a strong sense of fairness as mayor and treating all Chicagoans and their neighborhoods equally.

Yet others stressed the negative aspects of Daley's legacy, like the looming $655 million city budget deficit he left his successor. The Chicago Public Schools and the Chicago Transit Authority had deficits of hundreds of millions of dollars. In a stinging editorial, the *Chicago Tribune* pointed out that "Chicago is broke. For that, Daley is significantly responsible. He spent too much money fulfilling proud ambitions for his city. He awarded sweetheart labor contracts that extend years beyond his reign. And he let unfunded pension obligations metastasize to a potentially devastating $20 billion-with-a-b."[80] In summer of 2013, Moody's Investor Service downgraded Chicago's general obligation bond rating by three levels, and, in May 2015, once again to junk bond status.[81] Other negatives included his "boss" style of leadership, police brutality in the city, privatization deals like the parking meters that cheated taxpayers, overt patronage, scandals, and constant corruption. Under Daley's long tenure as mayor, the *Chicago Tribune* exposed "what appeared to be sweetheart fencing and janitorial contracts worth millions of dollars granted under questionable circumstances to companies with ties to the mayor or members of his family."[82]

CHAPTER FIVE

Fall from Grace

C hicago and Illinois at large may not be the best places for a young, up-and-coming individual to embark on a political career. There are good chances the person may pick up some bad habits, get tempted into doing mischievous things, and become ensnared in "a culture of political corruption" simply because Chicago is the most corrupt city in the United States, and Illinois is the third-most corrupt state, according to a report from the University of Illinois published by Professor Dick Simpson and his colleagues. According to the report and data published by the United States Department of Justice, from 1976 through 2018 "Chicago had a total of 1,750 public corruption convictions. For comparison, Los Angeles has seen 1,547 cases, while the New York City borough of Manhattan saw 1,360."[1] Illinois remains the third-most corrupt state, based on the formula that compares the number of each area's corruption convictions with its population.[2]

Unfortunately, through the years, a number of Latino politicians have lost their way. They got caught up in political corruption, embarrassed themselves and their families, ruined their careers, and some ended up serving time in jail. Many residents in the Latino community became disillusioned with Chicago's government because they had waited decades for meaningful political representation, only to see some of their elected officials disgracing themselves and being hauled off to jail for corruption.

Ambrosio Medrano — "I'm Not a Snitch"

Ambrosio Medrano served as an administrative assistant to Richard M. Daley while he was working as the state's attorney. In 1989, he was the Latino coordinator for Daley's successful mayoral campaign. He became the executive director of the Mayor's Commission of Latino Affairs. Later, with Daley's backing, Medrano was elected alderman of the Twenty-Fifth Ward in 1991.

He was a staunch supporter of Mayor Daley and his initiatives. He became the senior member of the Chicago City Council's Latino Caucus and chairman of the council's Housing Committee. Medrano earned his bachelor's degree in Human Services from Northeastern Illinois University (NEIU). Many other Latino politicians in Chicago also graduated from NEIU, which has a large Latino student population. Charismatic, and with an infectious smile, Medrano was a rising political star with a promising future. Residents of the Mexican enclave of Pilsen spoke highly of the alderman's efforts to improve city services in their neighborhood.

In 1996, Medrano had been alderman for nearly five years. Then, in January of 1996, he met with Federal Bureau of Investigation (FBI) agents who showed up at his City Hall office: "The agents then gave him a front-row seat to watch a video. Medrano had the starring role; the tape showed him accepting $1,000 from corrupt contractor and FBI 'mole' John Christopher. Medrano told the agents, 'You got me.'"[3] Medrano was the first conviction in a nine-year federal investigation of public corruption and an illegal dumping scheme called Operation Silver Shovel. Nineteen people were indicted in Silver Shovel, and only Twelfth Ward alderman Ray Frias was acquitted. One FBI agent hinted that if Medrano wore a wire for them to eavesdrop on other aldermen in the City Council, they might consider a reduction of his sentence. But Medrano refused. "I'm not a snitch," Medrano said. "It goes beyond that—you don't blame somebody else for your mistake."[4]

Medrano was hailed as a hero and stand-up guy by his colleagues in the City Council for refusing to wear a wire and snitch on others.[5] Medrano pleaded guilty to one count of bribery. He accepted $31,000 in bribes from John Christopher to allow him to illegally dump truckloads of waste and debris in his ward. He was sentenced to thirty months in prison and served his term at the Federal Work Camp at Oxford, Wisconsin. Medrano stated that he was a victim of racially selective enforcement by federal agents. Medrano said prosecutors solely targeted him and other minorities in Silver Shovel and other public corruption cases, "Why was it only blacks (and) a few Hispanics?" he said. Scott Lassar, United States attorney for the Northern District of Illinois, categorically denies that his office pursues race-based, selective prosecutions."[6]

After prison, Medrano struggled to find a full-time job. He had no money. He tried to win back his aldermanic Twenty-Fifth Ward seat. But the incumbent alderman, Danny Solis beat him. Obviously, Medrano did not learn his lesson after one stint in federal prison. In 2013, he was convicted of plotting to bribe a Los Angeles public official to obtain a government contract for a mail-order drug contract for business colleagues. He was convicted a third time for a scheme with Cook County Commissioner Joseph Moreno to sell bandages to public hospitals, including Cook County's Stroger Hospital.[7] Early in 2014, two federal judges handed Medrano a total of thirteen years in prison over corrupt deals involving bribes and kickbacks.[8] A federal judge told Medrano he had pulled off a corruption trifecta.[9] In May of 2020, due to the high risk of contracting COVID-19 behind bars, Medrano was released from prison. For the rest of his sentence, until September 2025, he will be on home confinement. Medrano was dubbed Illinois's first "three-time loser."

Joseph José Martinez—Free Taxpayer Money

When Mayor Jane M. Byrne handpicked Joseph José Martinez, Puerto Rican, as alderman of the Thirty-First Ward on December 11, 1981, he was hard pressed to say what he was going to do about the ward's problems, chief among them housing decay and high unemployment. He offered no specific program. Instead, he asked for his community's trust. Martinez had firm roots in the regular Democratic Organization. He worked faithfully for the Democratic Party for twelve years. During elections, he walked miles across the West Town and Humboldt Park neighborhoods to convince voters to support organization candidates—White candidates—even when the opposition was a fellow Puerto Rican trying to get a piece of the political pie.

While earning his law degree at night from DePaul University's College of Law, he was an administrative assistant for the Cook County Board of Appeals. Martinez appeared to be a serious man with a strong patriotic streak and a powerful belief in the American work ethic. "Nothing is given to anyone," Martinez said. "I've worked since the age of 12. I've struggled for 21 years in school. Nobody even gave me anything."[10] He later joined the law firm of Fourteenth Ward alderman Edward M. Burke. Youthful and aggressive, Martinez moved steadily up the organization ranks from precinct worker to community representative to precinct captain. He served, prepared, and waited for his opportunity. It came on December 11, 1981, when he was sworn in to replace alderman Chester Kuta, who unexpectedly resigned.

Shortly after becoming alderman, Martinez ended his first public interview with a promise, "There is nothing I will ever do to bring shame to Puerto Ricans," he said. "That is my promise and I aim to keep it."[11] Edward Nedza, a machine loyalist, was state senator of the Fifth District on the Northwest Side and committeeman of the Thirty-First Ward. Nedza maneuvered behind the scenes to get Martinez out and Miguel Santiago in. In 1983, Martinez announced that he would not seek reelection. Martinez disappeared from the political landscape for a while. But when he reappeared in public, he seemed to have forgotten his strong work ethic and his promise. In January of 1997, it was reported former alderman Joseph Martinez, 51, joined the list of officials snared in a federal probe of payroll padding. Martinez pleaded guilty to one count of fraud and of pocketing thousands of dollars in wages and benefits while doing no work.[12] Martinez became the twenty-seventh defendant charged in the three-year-long ghost-payrolling investigation.

Using a new name, "Martinez-Fraticelli," the former alderman actually worked for three different City Council committees, between 1989 and 1992, in which he did no work but pocketed $53,145 in pay and $37,352 in health insurance benefits in his ghost assignments. At the same time, he was earning more than $100,000 at Edward Burke's law firm.[13] Lawyers for Martinez alleged that alderman Burke gave Martinez the ghost jobs so the city would pick up the cost of health insurance that the law firm did not offer it employees. Edward Burke denied being part of the scheme. Lawyers for Martinez asked US District Judge Ruben Castillo that their client be given probation. But Judge Castillo—who is Puerto Rican and Mexican—disagreed and said, "Just think what message that would send. That's not going to happen with this type of ripoff, a ripoff that goes on for seven years."[14] In January 1998, Judge Castillo sentenced Martinez to five months in prison, five months of home confinement, one hundred hours of community service, and fined him $15,000.[15] Martinez eventually repaid the city $91,000. He was disbarred as a practicing attorney. But in May 2006, the Illinois Supreme Court ruled that Martinez could be reinstated to the state bar.[16]

Miriam Santos—"Time for People to Belly Up"

Miriam Santos was a young and quickly rising political star in the Democratic Party. She worked for Richard M. Daley when he was Cook County State's Attorney. After Daley was elected as mayor, he appointed Santos to the City Treasurer's position in 1989 to complete the term of former treasurer Cecil Partee. She won election to a full term as treasurer in 1991, becoming the first Latina elected to a citywide office in Chicago. She was reelected multiple times and served for ten years as city treasurer. Santos represented the American Dream for minority politicians. She worked her way up from working-class roots. One of five children of a Gary, Indiana, steelworker of Puerto Rican descent, she started public school in Gary without knowing English. Santos paid her way through college and law school by working full-time factory jobs in the evenings. In addition to a law degree, in 1990, she earned an MBA from Northwestern University.[17]

Santos was ambitious, fiercely independent, and outspoken. In a 1991 interview, Santos recalled that her parents taught her "that you could never compromise yourself, that you had to bring integrity and values to your workplace."[18] It seemed she was on a fast track to stardom. Many Latinos believed she had the skills and personality to someday become Chicago's first Latina mayor.[19] But in 1991, Santos accused Mayor's Daley's top advisers of harassing her, intruding on her statutory powers, and pressuring her to grease deals with politically connected pension fund investors. She publicly revealed that she refused to invest $5 million in pension funds in a South Loop hotel developed by Paul Stepan, Daley's chief fundraiser.[20] Mayor Daley became infuriated that Santos—someone he helped get ahead politically—would be disloyal and dare take him on and try to publicly embarrass him. Daley tried to get back at Santos by persuading the general assembly to approve a bill that removed the treasurer from two pension fund boards. But then Governor Jim Edgar vetoed the bill and rescued Santos.[21]

Some Latino politicians rallied to the defense of Santos in her bitter power struggle with Daley over control of employee pension funds. Juan Andrade, president of the Midwest Voter Registration and Education Project "denounced the Daley power play as an 'indefensible usurpation' of Santos' authority."[22] But other Latino politicians were uncomfortable that Santos was waging a media campaign against the politically powerful Mayor Daley. They did not think the public feud was good for Santos's career nor would it have a happy ending. In 1998, the politically ambitious Santos won the Democratic nomination for Illinois attorney general. She was taking on the popular incumbent Jim Ryan. But soon there were whispers that she was under investigation for campaign misconduct. Some of Santos's office workers publicly complained that she was a poor manager who was mercurial and unreasonable. They complained that under her leadership, the treasurer's office was a revolving door.

Workers stated that Santos was forcing them to do political campaign work on city time.

In May 1999, in a packed courtroom, Santos was convicted on five counts of mail fraud and one count of attempted extortion. Nine of her office's sixteen employees testified for the government at her trial. The jury convicted Santos of defrauding the city by cutting off business to seven brokerage firms that refused to make $10,000 contributions to her campaign for attorney general. During the trial, jurors heard a tape-recorded telephone conservation in which Santos pressured a broker from Fuji Securities for such a contribution. As the brief conversation with the Fuji broker neared an end Santos grew indignant and declared: "but this is not a choice. . . . Now it's time for people to belly up."[23] Two counts of mail fraud were related to her requiring treasurer's office employees to work on her attorney general campaign while on city time.

In July 1999, US District Judge Charles Norgle Sr. sentenced Miriam Santos to forty months in federal prison and ordered her to pay $53,000 in restitution. "I think your ambition created problems for you," Norgle told her when handing down the harsh sentence.[24] Before the sentencing, Santos told Norgle: "I deeply regret the pain and suffering that has been endured by my family, my friends, my community."[25] But the judge chastised Santos for not accepting responsibility for her wrongdoing. Santos served four months of the forty-month sentence before a federal appeals court overturned the conviction because of a "veritable avalanche of errors" in cross-examining witnesses and obtaining evidence at her first trial.

After being released from prison, Santos accused Daley and his advisers of being behind her conviction. "A defiant Santos told reporters that male politicians would not have gotten into trouble for what she did. 'I am probably the first woman who had to go to jail for PMS-ing,'" she said.[26] She reclaimed her city treasurer job. However, in October 2000, nearly two weeks before the start of her retrial, Santos pleaded guilty to only one count of mail fraud. She also resigned as city treasurer. Her bargain with the prosecutors included time already served in prison, paying $20,000 restitution to the city, and a $1,000 fine to the federal government. "This concludes my career as a public figure," Santos said after pleading guilty. "I am peaceful as I walk away." Santos then went the four blocks to City Hall, resigned, hugged some of her office workers and, brushing away tears, left in a waiting car.[27]

Rey Colón—One Too Many

Some Latino politicians did not get entangled in corruption and crime but instead got caught up in certain situations where embarrassing aspects of their private lives became public. They inadvertently aired their dirty laundry in public and it raised questions about their character and integrity. Former Thirty-Fifth Ward alderman Rey Colón was a case in point. Colón grew up in the Logan Square neighborhood. He graduated from Carl Schurz High School and graduated from Roosevelt University with a degree in community management. Colón worked for many years in the nonprofit sector providing diverse, quality social services for neighborhood residents. He worked as executive director of the Boys and Girls Clubs of Chicago and as area manager of the Chicago Park District. Later, he became executive director of the YMCA of Metropolitan Chicago.

Colón ran unsuccessfully for alderman of the Thirty-Fifth Ward against the incumbent Vilma Colom, who had close ties with Thirty-Third Ward alderman Richard F. Mell and other old-guard machine politicians. While Colón lost the election, he received an impressive 40 percent of the vote. After the election, Colón resumed his work with the YMCA. He facilitated a $7.5 million fundraising effort and directed the construction of the brand-new McCormick Tribune YMCA. The new YMCA in Logan Square opened its doors in December 2001. In 2003, Colón once again ran for alderman of the Thirty-Fifth Ward against the now eight-year incumbent Villma Colom. Colón portrayed himself as the progressive, grass-roots candidate, while his opponent was viewed as the machine candidate. This time, Colón won the February 25, 2003, election with 60 percent of the vote. He was regarded as a good alderman who consistently improved city services in the Logan Square neighborhood. Colón said, "I have been fortunate in securing public infrastructure improvements that have leveraged private investment. I've improved parks, attracted the construction of new academic institutions, and maintained a business-friendly environment that has spurred economic growth with hundreds of new jobs."[28]

After serving as alderman for thirteen years, however, some believed Colón had become complacent and was no longer progressive and independent in his thoughts and actions. Colón's reputation was badly tarnished when he was arrested by state police about 1 a.m. on a Friday in July 2014 on the Eisenhower Expressway and charged with driving under the influence of alcohol and driving with an expired license. The story and his police mug shot were in the major newspapers the next day. His eyes were red and he looked disheveled. The alderman refused to comment about the arrest; "It really doesn't help me to talk about details of the case because it's not something that needs to be tried in public," Colón said at City Hall.[29]

In early 2015, Colón was acquitted of the DUI charges. But his character was seriously damaged by all the negative publicity of his drunk driving arrest. Colón was seeking a fourth term. He was challenged by Carlos Ramirez-Rosa, a young, twenty-six-year-old progressive newcomer. Ramirez-Rosa was a former congressional caseworker for Rep. Luis Gutiérrez. "Rey Colón was an independent voice [on the council]—he's moved on from that," said Ramirez-Rosa.[30] Many did not believe the young, inexperienced Ramirez-Rosa could beat Colón. But in February 2015, Ramirez-Rosa when on to beat Colón by a wide margin to become the new alderman of the Thirty-Fifth Ward. Ramirez-Rosa had 67 percent of the vote to Colón's 33 percent, making it the only 2015 race in which an incumbent lost outright without a runoff.[31] Ramirez-Rosa said that his "parents were public school teachers, so quality schooling has always been important to [him]."[32] He was endorsed and supported by the powerful Chicago Teachers Union. Ramirez-Rosa became the first openly gay Latino alderman and the council's first Democratic Socialist.

Joseph Mario Moreno—"I Just Want to Be a Pig"

Former Cook County Board Commissioner Joseph Mario Moreno always seemed to be in a hurry, as if he was rushing from one important meeting to another. He gave the impression that he was a very busy businessman who had little time for small talk. He was always well dressed and preferred dark, expensive suits, silk ties, and shining black leather shoes. He served as a board member on numerous public and private businesses and government entities. The *Chicago Tribune* noted that "Moreno, 61, had a rags-to-riches story as one of four children raised in the Back of the Yards neighborhood by a mother who worked two jobs to keep food on the table after his father died in a work-related accident. Moreno built a law practice, was elected to the Cook County Board in 1994 and eventually earned more than $200,000 a year, lived in a million-dollar home and owned vacation property in Mexico."[33]

Moreno earned his law degree from DePaul University. He had big political ambitions. He ran for town president of the suburb of Cicero, Illinois, in the 2001 and 2003 municipal elections. He projected himself as a progressive, independent candidate who would clean up the longtime political corruption in Cicero. He thought he could beat the controversial Cicero town president Betty Loren-Maltese. However, in his first race Loren-Maltese soundly defeated him. "I ran alone in that election," Moreno says. "No one supported me because no one thought I could win."[34] In 2003, Moreno again ran for town president, and received endorsements from many Democratic politicians including Cook County Commissioner Roberto Maldonado and state Representative Willie Delgado. However, to Moreno's disappointment, former Rep. Luis Gutiérrez endorsed Ramiro Gonzalez, the Republican candidate, who beat Moreno to become town president.[35]

Moreno served on the Cook County Board from 1994 to 2013 and began drawing pension benefits in 2012 two years after he left office following his defeat to former state senator Jesús García. Despite the political setbacks, Moreno still enjoyed a good, comfortable life. He was married and had a family. But in 2012, Moreno was indicted on corruption charges for allegedly masterminding at least nine separate schemes involving kickbacks, bribes, and tax evasion, among other accusations, over three years. In July 2013, Moreno pleaded guilty of using his position on the Cook County Board to force a company with a county contract to subcontract some of the work to a company called Chicago Medical Equipment and Supply, which was owned by Moreno's friend Ron Garcia. Garcia was paying part of the profits from the deal back to Moreno. He also pleaded guilty to trying to force the Cook County hospital system to buy thousands of bandages from a company that was going to give Moreno five dollars for each bandage purchased. That deal involved former Chicago alderman Ambrosio Medrano.

Moreno admitted accepting an envelope with a $5,000 cash bribe to support construction of a waste transfer station in Cicero. In an FBI undercover recording of the bribe, Moreno delivered his infamous quote, "I don't want to be a hog; I just want to be a pig," said Moreno, then a volunteer member of the town's economic development panel; "Hogs get slaughtered; pigs get fat."[36] In February 2014, Medrano was sentenced to eleven years in prison, ordered to forfeit $100,000 and pay a total of more than $138,000 in restitution. United States district judge Gary Feinerman said, "Mr. Moreno was not a reluctant participant in these schemes; he was an active participant. Moreno 'embraced them with gusto and pursued them with vigor.'"[37] In a packed courtroom of family and friends, Moreno asked his attorney to read a three-page letter he wrote to the judge. Moreno said that "He had served 'honorably' for most of his career but then made 'bad choices' about who he associated with. . . . 'I suffered from the flawed traits of excess pride, greed, selfishness and a sense of invincibility. . . . I stand before you a disgraced man.'"[38] In March 2014, to the chagrin of Moreno's ex-wife, Nancy, federal prosecutors seized Moreno's pension benefits to satisfy a $134,192 lien the federal government placed on Moreno over unpaid taxes.[39]

Proco "Joe" Moreno—Someone Stole My Car

Former First Ward alderman Proco "Joe" Moreno was never involved in any dramatic public corruption scandals that have plagued other Chicago aldermen. But he, like other Latino aldermen, got caught up in certain situations where embarrassing aspects of their private lives became public. He had a tendency to air his dirty laundry in public and it raised questions about his judgment and character. Moreno was appointed to the City Council by then mayor Richard M. Daley in 2010, when then First Ward alderman Manny Flores took a job heading the Illinois Commerce Commission. He was elected the following year by a wide margin. Moreno was a graduate of Metropolitan Leadership Institute, which trained and educated future young Latino leaders in the city. The Institute was run by the United Neighborhood Organization, a powerful Latino educational and political group closely allied with Daley.

Moreno soon earned a reputation for acting like a big-shot politico and being overly confrontational in the City Council and with people in general. The *Chicago Tribune* pointed out that "Moreno has positioned himself as a pragmatic progressive on the council. He has championed causes such as a higher minimum wage and the elimination of plastic shopping bags at Chicago grocery stores, but also clashed with the Progressive Caucus bloc of aldermen, who he says are sometimes needlessly obstructionist and don't offer solutions."[40] In 2017, Moreno was caught on video threatening and taunting the owner of the Bucktown building that housed the famed Double Door music club after the building owner had evicted the club owners.

In June 2018, Moreno confronted a woman who, he said, had parked illegally in a bicycle lane on North Clark Street. Moreno said the woman's car was also blocking him from parking, and he asked her to move closer to the curb. He then showed her his City Council badge, which resembled a police badge, but identifies the holder as a member of the council. "I told her, well, in Chicago, you get a ticket for parking in a bike lane," he said.[41] The woman called the police to charge that Moreno yelled at her and was posing as a cop to force her to move. Moreno said he never told her he was a cop. The Chicago police investigated whether Moreno was impersonating a police officer and they concluded he only showed the woman his aldermanic badge. No one was charged in the incident. But many wondered why aldermen needed badges.

In February 2019, the *Chicago Sun-Times* endorsed Moreno for reelection but with an interesting caveat, "Four years ago, we endorsed Proco "Joe" Moreno for re-election but said he can be an annoying guy, we're doing it again. . . . Dial it down, man. No, that woman should not have parked in the bike lane last June, but flashing your goofy alderman's badge and yelling at her was silly."[42] The slew of public scandals hurt Moreno's chances of being reelected. In February of 2019, Moreno lost his bid for reelection to newcomer and Democratic Socialist Daniel La Spata, who was backed by the Democratic Socialists of America—La Spata won 61 percent of the vote while Moreno won only 38.9 percent.

Then, in May 2019, Moreno was in the news again when he was arrested by Chicago police and charged with insurance fraud, disorderly conduct, obstruction of justice, and falsely reporting a vehicle stolen. He spent a night in jail. Apparently, Moreno had called the police to report that his leased black 2016 Audi A6 sedan had been stolen from his Bucktown home. A month later police arrested thirty-five-year-old Liliya Hrabar, who was driving the car. Distraught and crying Hrabar explained to police that Moreno and she were dating and he had let her use the car. Police discovered that the night before he reported the car stolen, Moreno had invited Hrabar over to his house, gave her the keys to the car, took her to his garage, and watched her drive away.[43] Police determined the luxury sports sedan had not been stolen at all.

Meanwhile, Moreno called his insurance company to report his car had been stolen from his garage. Based on that claim, the insurance company was poised to pay $30,000 to cover the loss of the vehicle. Liliya Hrabar filed a defamation suit against Moreno.[44] Moreno walked out of the Leighton Criminal Court Building in May 2019, after Judge John Fitzgerald Lyke Jr. ordered him released on his own recognizance, noting that the charges showed a "terrible lapse in judgment."[45] While his first case was still pending, in December 2020, Moreno was charged with several additional misdemeanors—DUI and reckless driving—after his Audi rammed and sideswiped at least eight cars along four blocks in the Gold Coast neighborhood before smashing into a tree on a Sunday night.[46] An angry judge immediately ordered that Moreno be placed in the Cook County jail for a week. The judge also ordered that upon release, Moreno enter into an alcohol rehabilitation program. On July 16, 2021, Moreno was sentenced to two years of probation after he pleaded guilty to obstruction of justice and disorderly conduct charges for falsely reporting his car stolen. The DUI and other misdemeanor charges were still pending in traffic court.

Ricardo Muñoz — The Next Chapter

Former longtime Twenty-Second Ward alderman Ricardo Muñoz unfortunately ended his long political career with unsavory aspects of his private life becoming public. When marital problems and allegations of domestic violence against his wife became public, combined with a federal indictment for stealing city funds, they left a dark cloud over Muñoz's exceptional political career. Chicago's two major newspapers had regarded Muñoz as one of the City Council's most progressive, effective aldermen, and they repeatedly endorsed him for reelection. Muñoz was born in Monterrey, Mexico. His family immigrated to the United States and settled on the Near West Side of Chicago. Later, the family moved to the Little Village neighborhood. Muñoz was appointed to his seat by then mayor Richard M. Daley in 1993. He rose from a troubled past as a teenager to become chief of staff to then alderman Jesús García. When García won election as a state senator, he asked Mayor Daley to appoint Muñoz to replace him. Daley did so and hailed Muñoz as a positive role model for youth.[47] At the age of 27, Muñoz was then the youngest member of the City Council.

However, the young alderman came with a checkered past. Muñoz was open about his former teenage ties to gangs in Little Village. He also had disclosed that during his teenage years he had been arrested three times for two weapons violations and one charge of possession of controlled substances. For each offense, he was given a year of court supervision.

Despite his troubled years as a teenager, Muñoz earned a college degree at Northern Illinois University. He became the city's longest tenured Latino alderman. He was viewed as a progressive, independent alderman who was not afraid to speak his mind or to vote against mayoral policies that he did not think were in the best interests of his constituents. He defined a progressive politician as one "who is interested in helping working-class people better themselves, instead of looking out for your own interests."[48]

Muñoz explained that he loved his many years serving his mostly Mexican constituents as alderman. He helped improve city services throughout his ward. He devoted a lot of time in his ward organizing block clubs, and weekly cleanups of streets, alleys, and vacant lots. He is especially proud that he was able to assist in the construction of two new Chicago Public Library branches, three new elementary schools, and two new high schools in his ward. "It's important to have Latino representation in the Chicago City Council. You need Latino elected officials to speak up for the needs of the community," said Muñoz. "You hope they bring improved city services to their constituents and important projects like new schools and libraries."[49]

But Muñoz faced other controversies over the years. He intervened to help his daughter get into a prestigious city high school in 2009. And in 2008, his estranged father was sentenced to four years in prison for taking part in a fake identification (fake ID) ring. In 2010, six months before the City Council election, he said he was an alcoholic, admitting he drank excessively after work but not in the mornings and afternoons.[50] Yet despite his personal problems, Muñoz kept getting himself reelected as aldermen.

In July of 2018, Muñoz said that he would not seek reelection. At the time he said he was retiring because he was "having fun writing the next chapter of my life."[51] However in early January 2019, Muñoz was arrested at his ward office on a misdemeanor domestic battery charge stemming from an alleged New Year's Eve altercation with his wife. His wife, Betty Torres-Muñoz, alleged Muñoz was intoxicated when the incident occurred. She filed a petition for an order of protection saying she and her husband got into a heated argument and that Muñoz grabbed her and pushed her backward, causing her to hit her back and head and twist her arm.[52] Muñoz's wife also said that "her husband had been abusive previously, and she accused him of being an 'addict' and a 'womanizer.'"[53] Their divorce is pending.[54]

Then, in April 2019, it was alleged that during the time Muñoz was head of the City Council's Progressive Reform Caucus, he made unauthorized expenses of $36,849 for personal expenses. Reached by a reporter, Muñoz said, "I'm paying it back . . . and Muñoz has paid back $24,900 thus far."[55] However, in April 2021, Muñoz was indicted by federal prosecutors on fifteen counts of wire fraud and one count of money laundering for allegedly stealing almost $38,000 from the accounts of the Progressive Reform Caucus on personal expenses for sport tickets, travel, meals, skydiving, hotels, and personal items at a suburban Lover's Lane. Muñoz pleaded guilty to stealing the money and in March 2022, a federal judge sentenced Muñoz to 13 months in jail.

Luis Arroyo—"This Is the Jackpot"

Political corruption is not just limited to the Chicago City Council, it reaches all levels of government in Illinois. For example, Illinois state representative Luis Arroyo, a Chicago Democrat who was an assistant majority leader, was charged in a federal criminal complaint of bribery in late October 2019. He resigned in disgrace the following month, just one week after his arrest and just hours before a legislative committee was set to consider his ouster from the General Assembly.[56] According to federal charges, Arroyo allegedly offered to pay a state senator $2,500 a month in kickbacks in exchange for support on legislation involving gambling sweepstakes games that would benefit one of Arroyo's private lobbying clients. The senator was wearing a wire for the FBI when Arroyo delivered the first of the $2,500 checks at a restaurant in Skokie. "This is, this is the jackpot" the complaint quoted Arroyo telling the senator as he handed over the check.[57]

The *Chicago Tribune* identified the senator whom Arroyo was accused of trying to bribe as Terry Link (D-Vernon Hills), although Link denied being the cooperating witness.[58] Federal authorities alleged that Arroyo then promised the senator that he would give him additional payments over the next six to twelve months. Arroyo pleaded not guilty to the bribery charge.[59] In August 2020, federal authorities charged Link with filing a false income tax return for the year 2016 in which he claimed his income was $265,450 even though it was much higher than that.[60] A month later, Link resigned the Senate seat he had held for more than two decades. He pleaded guilty to filing a false income tax return.

Arroyo was another Latino politician who came from humble beginnings and became a successful rising star. After earning his GED, his family opened the popular Arroyo's restaurant on the Northwest Side of Chicago. He then worked for the city of Chicago. Arroyo was a high school dropout. He was born in Puerto Rico and came to Chicago as a boy with his family. He became a Water Department bricklayer but rose to power through the Democratic Party to become a well-known politician in North Side Latino politics.[61] Arroyo's son, Luis Arroyo Jr., is a Cook County commissioner.

Arroyo did early work for former Mayor Jane M. Byrne, and later former US Rep. Luis Gutiérrez. Arroyo was first appointed as Illinois state Representative for the Third District in 2006. He was reelected six times. He served on numerous committees in the General Assembly and was able to bring millions of dollars for improvements of schools, parks, and high schools in his district. On November 15, Eva-Dina Delgado was appointed to serve the remainder of Arroyo's term. The appointment sparked controversy as Arroyo also served as Thirty-Sixth Ward committeeman and cast his vote in the appointment process. Other politicians wanted Arroyo to abstain from the process, but he allowed neighboring Thirtieth Ward committeeman Ariel Reboyras to act as his proxy. Delgado is a lawyer and former lobbyist. Much of her lobbying was done in Springfield for Mayor Richard M. Daley. "I consider myself a person . . . of great integrity," Delgado said.[62] As for Arroyo's legacy, one columnist opined, "'recklessly corrupt' is definitely what I would call someone who threw away their future by handling over a $2,500 check to an FBI informant."[63] A federal indictment later added new wire and mail fraud charges against Arroyo. In November 2021, Arroyo pleaded guilty to most of the allegations. In May 2022 he was sentenced to 57 months in prison.

Martin Sandoval — "I'll Go Balls to the Wall"

In September 2019, FBI agents raided the Springfield and Cicero offices and the Southwest Side home of Illinois state senator Martin Sandoval, who was chair of the Senate's Transportation Committee. Sandoval soon learned he was the first person caught in a wide-ranging FBI investigation of political corruption in Illinois. In their raids on Sandoval's offices and home, the *Chicago Tribune* stated, "Federal agents sought information on construction magnates, transportation officials, lobbyist, and power company bigwigs. It included a video gambling and racetrack boss, a clout-heavy red light camera company, a member of the tollway board, and at least three suburban mayors."[64]

Sandoval was born in the Back of the Yards neighborhood on Chicago's Southwest Side. He received a Roman Catholic education deeply steeped in religious teachings. He graduated from Archbishop Quigley Preparatory

Seminary South High School and earned a bachelor's degree at Loyola University Chicago. He first won election to the Senate in 2002 with the support of former Mayor Richard M. Daley. Soon after the raids, federal prosecutors alleged that Senator Sandoval took a bribe to oppose legislation that would harm the red-light camera industry, specifically the clout-heavy red light camera company, SafeSpeed. As a result of the ongoing investigation, Sandoval resigned from office in January 2020. That same month during a lengthy hearing in federal court, Sandoval pleaded guilty to bribery and tax charges and was cooperating in the investigation. "He admitted to taking $20,000 in campaign contributions and later $70,000 cash from a SafeSpeed co-owner who was secretly working with agents."[65]

In court, it was revealed just how greedy Sandoval had gotten. He complained to one SafeSpeed representative in 2018 that he wanted more in bribe money. He argued that as the head of the Senate's Transportation Committee, he was the one sticking out his neck on behalf of the company in Springfield. Yet SafeSpeed was giving more lucrative deals to other politically connected "consultants," cutting them in on a percentage of the camera revenue that kept cash rolling in every month. Sandoval told the representative, who was secretly recording the conversation for the FBI, "So why don't I get that offer?" Sandoval griped. "'Cause you know I'll go balls to the wall for anything you ask . . . It's hard for me to swallow how (people) make so much off you. Right? And I gotta do the work."[66]

In court, Sandoval also revealed that he had taken more than $250,000 in bribes from other people, dating back to at least 2016, in exchange for using his Senate position to promote their interests. As he left the courthouse Sandoval told reporters he was ashamed and took full responsibility for his actions. "I apologize to the people of Illinois and most important the constituents that I've served over the last 17 years," he said.[67] In December 2020, Martin Sandoval, fifty-six, died of COVID-19.

Daniel Solis — "A Nice Ending"

When Ambrosio Medrano, former alderman of the Twenty-Fifth Ward was indicted for corruption for the third time, the new alderman, Daniel "Danny" Solis said, "Sometimes you think it's easy to get away with things and that people won't find out. But, in this day and age, with all the indictments and convictions, you got to be crazy to even contemplate that."[68] It is too bad that Solis did not take his own advice. In January 2019, a bombshell revelation became public indicating that the powerful Twenty-Fifth Ward alderman Daniel Solis spent two years cooperating with the FBI as part of a public corruption investigation. Reportedly, Solis secretly recorded conversations to help support the FBI's investigation of Edward Burke, alderman of the Fourteenth Ward. In November 2018, FBI agents raided Burke's offices at City Hall, and later his ward office. Then, in January 2019, federal prosecutors charged Burke with attempted extortion for allegedly trying to pressure executives of a Burger King franchise in his ward to give him legal work in return for his help obtaining a permit they needed.[69] Four months later, Burke was hit with a fourteen-count racketeering and extortion indictment accusing him of using his governmental role to muscle business for his law firm.[70] Solis also secretly made video recordings of the once-powerful former Illinois House Speaker Michael Madigan. In March 2022, a federal grand jury indicted Madigan and charged him with a racketing conspiracy, using interstate facilities for bribery, wire fraud, and attempted extortion.

Several of Solis's colleagues in the City Council were dismayed and felt betrayed that he would secretly record them for the FBI and try to catch them in wrongdoing. "Where I come from, if you wear a wire someone's going to kick your ass," said Southwest Side alderman Matt O'Shea, Nineteenth Ward.[71] Daniel Solis was appointed alderman by Mayor Daley after Ambrosio Medrano pleaded guilty to corruption charges. Solis served for twenty-two years in the City Council and is the second longest serving Latino in the council. In November 2018, Solis announced he would not seek reelection. Solis got his start in politics as an activist and protestor in the 1970s who criticized administrators at the University of Illinois Chicago over low Latino enrollment. He later helped start an alternative high school for dropouts. He was a cofounder of the United Neighborhood Organization (UNO) in the early 1980s, a Saul Alinsky-style nonprofit group that trained lay Latino leaders. Later UNO and Solis forged close ties with Daley and Mayor Rahm Emanuel.[72]

UNO created the supposedly independent UNO Charter School Network and then used good old-fashioned clout to get a $98 million state grant to build charter schools. UNO's former CEO Juan Rangel engaged in "pinstripe patronage" and gave million-dollar school construction contracts to two brothers of his top deputy Miguel d'Escoto and other close friends. State and federal officials investigated the nepotism and patronage. UNO settled civil charges of defrauding bond investors in a federal case brought by the

US Securities and Exchange Commission. Rangel was forced to step down as CEO of the Charter School Network.[73]

Many political observers wondered why Solis was wearing a wire for the FBI—they soon found out. A court filing made public in March 2019, showed the FBI spent more than two years investigating alleged corruption schemes by Solis, secretly listening in on thousands of phone calls as the alderman solicited favors, campaign donations, and sexual services at a massage parlor. Solis was chairman of the City Council's Zoning Committee, and regularly asked developers seeking his zoning help for campaign donations. He threw a fancy party for his son at the Indiana farm formerly owned by Oprah Winfrey. The farm was now owned by a real estate developer who regularly had business before Solis's committee.[74] The real estate developer usually charged $20,000 to rent the farm for a day, but he did not charge Solis anything. For years, Solis was criticized by Pilsen residents for being too cozy with the real estate developers that were changing the neighborhood's character through gentrification.[75]

Solis also paid himself more than $330,000 from a Twenty-Fifth Ward campaign fund that he chaired—he received regular checks for what was labeled simply "services rendered" or "contractual work."[76] The affidavit alleged that Solis accepted erectile dysfunction drugs and sexual services in exchange for his help with official city business. As *Chicago Tribune* reporters explained, "Federal authorities captured several conversations in which Solis sought Viagra—including once before a trip to Taiwan—from political consultant Roberto Caldero, who at the time was representing a street sweeping company that was looking for a financial break from the city. . . . Solis asked Caldero for the drug on at least four different occasions."[77] The affidavit suggested that Caldero also offered prostitution services to Solis at a North Side massage parlor on several occasions. "Let me tell you why I called," Solis was quoted as saying in one call from July 2015, "I want to get a good massage, with a nice ending." When Caldero said he knew of a place and would make an appointment, Solis asked, "What kind of women do they got there," the affidavit said. "Asian," Caldero responded. "Oh good! Good, good, good," Solis said, according to a transcript. "I like Asian."[78]

Caldero was a longtime political operative for former US Rep. Luis Gutiérrez going back to Gutiérrez's first run for the Chicago City Council in the 1980s. The Chicago Board of Ethics fined Roberto Caldero $25,000 for failing to register as a lobbyist. And in February 2021, Caldero was charged in a scheme to steer a Chicago Public Schools $1 billion custodial contract to a Cleveland-based company in exchange for donations to Solis's campaign. Caldero was subsequently charged in an eight-count indictment with wire fraud, federal program bribery and facilitating bribery. Also caught up in the ongoing public corruption probes was former state Rep. Edward Acevedo, Second District, who served in the Illinois House from 1995 to 2017. Acevedo was charged with failing to file tax returns for four years. Acevedo initially pleaded not guilty.[79] However, he later pleaded guilty to the charges and in March 2022, a federal judge handed a six-month prison sentence to Acevedo for not paying taxes on $37,000 over three years.

Disgraced former Chicago alderman Daniel Solis collects a nearly $95,000 annual (taxpayer-funded) city pension despite his role as a central figure in an ongoing public corruption scandal at City Hall.[80] By cooperating with the FBI, Solis was hoping to avoid facing any criminal charges against him that might lead to prison time.[81] In April 2022, federal prosecutors charged Solis with one count of bribery, but the prosecutors also announced that Solis had reached a deferred prosecution agreement with the US Attorney's office to keep him from going to jail. Solis has not been seen in public since being exposed as an FBI mole.

Bad Politicians?

Congressman Jesús García explained that he becomes angered when Latino politicians become corrupt. "To a large degree it taints all of us," said García, "and it has the potential for people seeing us in that light that all politicians are crooked and Latinos may not be any different than anyone else. So you get painted with a wide, broad brush and it's sad."[82] Gilbert Villegas, Thirty-Sixth Ward alderman, chairman of the Latino Caucus in the City Council, and former floor leader for Mayor Lori Lightfoot, agreed it is unfortunate to see Latino politicians get caught up in corruption. But he argued that there are bad people in all professions, not just politics. "What's the old saying? 'Power tends to corrupt and absolute power corrupts absolutely.' When you're in a powerful position, there's a lot of responsibilities and so people tend to gravitate towards you," said Villegas. "It's important that you have a group of people that will keep you grounded. You have bad priests, bad politicians, bad everything. There are going to be bad politicians, whether it be African American, Latino, Caucasian. I mean, if someone's bad, they are bad, period."[83]

It is not clear why some of these Latino politicians became corrupt over the years. Some of them obviously became greedy and wanted money and some had blind ambitions for higher office. Some politicians were in office for too many years and got comfortable believing no one was looking at them. These longtime politicians believed they did not have to be accountable to the public anymore, and that they could engage in corruption and would not get caught. Moreover, Chicago aldermen traditionally have had "aldermanic prerogative," and immense, unchecked power in their wards, especially in regard to development, granting building permits, and zoning changes. Consequently, aldermen, who already make more than $110,000 per year, become susceptible to taking bribes from businesses and developers seeking certain development and zoning changes in their wards. Since 1973, thirty-seven Chicago aldermen have pleaded guilty or have been convicted of crimes for various schemes to use the powers of their office to enrich themselves.

Moreover, some political observers believe that the Chicago City Council is too large, unwieldy, and that fifty aldermen are unnecessary. A smaller council of twenty-five aldermen could still effectively represent citizens and probably eliminate much aldermanic corruption. Most current aldermen, of course, have resisted attempts to curtail their aldermanic privileges and prerogatives, reduce their numbers, or reduce the countless committees with big budgets that they control.

One of the two steel, 59-foot Puerto Rican flags on Paseo Boricua on Division Street. One flag is near Western Avenue, shown here, and the other is about six blocks west on California Avenue. Photo by Wilfredo Cruz.

Mayor Richard M. Daley. Courtesy Harold Washington Library Center, Municipal Reference Library.

Virginia Martinez, lead attorney for the Mexican American Legal Defense and Educational Fund, in the early 1980s. Courtesy Virginia Martinez.

A collection of buttons from many political campaigns in Chicago through the years. Author's collection.

Patricia Mendoza is an associate judge for the Circuit Court of Cook County. She worked in the Juvenile Justice Division, First Municipal Division Traffic Court and the Domestic Violence Court. She was also regional counsel for the Mexican American Legal Defense and Educational Fund. Courtesy Patricia Mendoza.

Former Illinois state Senator Miguel del Valle (with tie) met with Latino seniors in the Illinois General Assembly chambers in Springfield, Illinois. The seniors visited the senator during a lobby day in 1987. Courtesy Miguel del Valle.

A Mexican Independence parade travels along Twenty-sixth Street and South Kedzie Avenue in Little Village in the early 1990s. There are more than 1,400 small businesses on the street, mostly Mexican-owned. The iconic street arch says, "Bienvenidos a Little Village." Courtesy *La Raza*.

Former Illinois state Senator Jesús García with children in the early 1990s. The children are from El Hogar Del Nino, a day care center in Pilsen. Courtesy Jesús García.

Outer lobby of the Mayor's Office on the fifth floor of City Hall. Portraits of all the individuals who served as mayor of Chicago. Photo by Wilfredo Cruz.

Left to right, Jesús García, U.S. presidential candidate Barack Obama, and Twenty-Fifth Ward Alderman Ricardo Muñoz in Chicago in 2007. García and Muñoz were holding a fundraising for Obama in his first run for president. Courtesy Ricardo Muñoz.

Left to right, first row, Beatriz Fausto-Sandoval, won election as a judge on Cook County's 14th subcircuit, Alma Anaya was elected Cook County Commissioner, and Aaron Ortiz won election as Illinois state Rep, First District all in 2018. *Back row,* U.S. Rep.-elect Jesús García and U.S. Senator Bernie Sanders (D-Vermont). Courtesy Ricardo Muñoz.

Above left, Tanya Patiño challenged Edward Burke for alderman of the 14th Ward in 2019. However, Patino was not able to unseat Burke, the longest serving alderman in the Chicago City Council. Photo by Wilfredo Cruz. *Above right,* Celina Villanueva was sworn into the Ill. House of Representatives in July 2018 to fill a vacancy. On Jan. 7, 2020 she was appointed to become Illinois state Senator of the 11th District after Martin Sandoval's resignation amid a corruption probe. Photo by Wilfredo Cruz.

Andre Vasquez, newly elected Socialist alderman of the 40th Ward, with Jessica Peters, his campaign manager and now his chief of staff. Photo by Wilfredo Cruz.

Top left, Rossana Rodríguez-Sanchez, newly elected Socialist alderman of the 33rd Ward. Photo by Wilfredo Cruz. *Top right*, Anna M. Valencia, City Clerk of Chicago. She was sworn into office on January 2017. Courtesy Travis Truitt. Photo by Monica Westlake, Columbia College, *The Chronicle*. *Right*, Mayor Eugene Sawyer. Courtesy Harold Washington Library Center, Municipal Reference Library.

CHAPTER SIX

Progressives, Socialists, and Machine Politicians

S ince about 2015, a new crop of young, fresh Latino faces has emerged on the political landscape. They have attempted to get themselves elected to political office by challenging old-guard, machine politicians who have been in office for decades. These younger opponents bring a refreshing energy and enthusiasm to city and state politics. Some call themselves independent and progressive and argue that machine politicians have been in office too long, are conservative in their viewpoints, and are out of touch with their constituents. Others call themselves Democratic Socialists and bring big ideas of using political office to pass legislation that helps working-class people with issues like affordable housing, a working wage, better education, rent control, and other important bread-and-butter issues. Some of these new faces have been able to beat great odds and have ousted old school Chicago politicians. Others have failed to win elected office but put up a good fight. They seem to represent a new era in Chicago politics.

Aarón Ortíz—Knocking on Doors

In the 2018 Democratic primary, Aarón Ortíz, a twenty-six-year-old political newcomer decided to challenge incumbent Daniel J. Burke for state Representative of Illinois's First District. Ortíz was part of a slate of Latino candidates backed by US Rep. elect Jesús García and US senator Bernie Sanders (D-VT). Ortíz was taking on Burke, who had been in office for twenty-eight years and was the brother of powerful Fourteenth Ward alderman Edward Burke. Daniel Burke was first elected to office before Ortíz was even born. But Ortíz believed that Burke was burnt out and was no longer addressing the needs of residents as the Southwest Side district changed from majority Eastern European to 68 percent Latino, predominately Mexican. "You got to be visible and accessible and leading on issues and supporting the Latino community. Burke wasn't necessarily being a leader on policy issues that affected the Latino community," said Aarón Ortíz.[1]

Very few people gave Ortíz a chance of winning. He was new to politics, had no political experience, and no name recognition. Daniel Burke suggested that Ortíz was far too green to do the job. "I have no issue with people of the majority seeking public office, but not characters like this Mr. Ortíz," Dan Burke says. "He knows no one in the whole legislative process. It's kind of bizarre."[2] Yet, in a stunning upset, Ortíz defeated Daniel Burke, winning 53 percent of votes compared to Burke's 46 percent—a difference of about 700 votes. "I honestly believe that the seven-hundred vote difference was due to me knocking on doors every single day," said Ortíz. "Campaigning a lot and knocking on doors in Gage Park or as far west as Garfield Ridge, or Stickney."[3] As he was knocking on doors some residents teased him about his youth and baby-face and jokingly asked if he was even old enough to vote. Other residents were impressed with his ideas and determination.

Ortíz could not believe he won, yet he was very happy about winning. "I feel excited, proud. It was such a huge win for the Latino community and that's what made it even more prideful," said Ortíz. "The community didn't have representation from the former state representative."[4] Winning political seats at the state level is especially important for Latinos as these seats often lead to being elected to even higher office. Ortíz becomes the youngest member of the Illinois General Assembly. In his campaign, Ortíz had the support and money and troops from Jesús García and organizations like United Working Families, the Chicago Teachers Union, some public sector unions, the Twenty-Second Ward Independent Political Organization, and an army of friends and volunteers.

At the same time that Ortíz won, two young Latinas also won elected office: Alma Anaya, 28, a García aide, won against Angie Sandoval, the daughter of state Senator Martin Sandoval, to replace García as Cook County commissioner; and Beatriz Fausto-Sandoval, 37, won to become the first Latina judge on Cook County's Fourteenth subcircuit. The *Chicago Reader* dubbed the three winners as "Latino Berniecrats," meaning that they support the ideas of US senator Bernie Sanders—ideas such as economic equality, labor rights, workplace democracy, universal health care, and immigrant rights.[5] García proudly appeared on television holding a broom to indicate a clean sweep. He expressed excitement about the emergence of new, younger Latinos on the political scene; "It's a new day and will get even better once we get alderman Edward Burke out of office," said Jesús García.[6]

Ortíz believes that he and the other newly elected Latinos officials represent a new generation of young, independent, progressively thinking politicians. "I definitely think that. I think progressive politics is really just advocating for the needs of your communities to be able to progress forward . . . for the progress of humanity, for the progress of low-income communities who have been marginalized. Not just for the Latino community, but again, for working-class families in general."[7] Ortíz was born in Chicago to immigrant parents from Durango, Mexico. His father was a forklift operator and his mother a school lunch lady. He grew up in the Gage Park neighborhood. He was a college counselor and soccer coach at Back of the Yards College Prep High School. He earned a bachelor's degree at the University of Illinois at Urbana-Champaign.

Ortíz won reelection in 2020. He was endorsed by the *Chicago Sun-Times* which said, "Given his background in education, it's not surprising he managed to direct $900,000 from last year's capital bill to Curie High School in Archer Heights to pay for building improvements. Other schools in his district also benefited from the bill. Long-term, Ortíz has the makings of an effective legislator."[8] Ortíz introduced a bill in the Illinois General Assembly in February 2020, to increase financial aid for prospective public school teachers and bilingual high school students. The bill would provide a yearly $5,000 college grant for up to eight hundred high school students who graduate with a state seal of biliteracy, as measured by standardized tests administered by the state. "There are many students of color, many of them bilingual, who face challenges accessing a public education, specifically around affordability," Ortíz said. "This bill tries to address that."[9]

In June 2019, Latino politicians, including Ortíz complained about judicial appointments made by Illinois Supreme Court justice Anne Burke, wife of indicted Fourteenth Ward alderman Edward Burke. They complained about Anne Burke's appointment of Daniel Tiernan, who is White, to fill a vacancy in a Fourteenth subcircuit dominated by Latinos. "It's important to have people in these positions that are not only qualified but also share the same experience as people they're elected—or, in this case, appointed—to serve," Ortíz said.[10]

In 2020, the up-and-coming Ortíz ran against alderman Edward Burke—the longest serving alderman in the City Council—for his Fourteenth Ward Democratic committeeman's seat. Again, he was viewed as the underdog. Edward

Burke had been committeeman since 1968 and had a campaign war chest of over $8 million. But again, Ortíz pulled out an upset and beat Burke; Ortíz received 40 percent of the vote compared to Burke's 33 percent, a margin of 392 votes. A third candidate, Alicia Elena Martinez, had 27 percent of the vote. Martinez was seen as a candidate put up by Burke to divide the Latino vote and pave the way for his reelection.[11]

The committeeman position was a longtime mark of party power, allowing the fifty ward bosses to control patronage armies who worked hard to protect their seats and those of preferred Democratic candidates by bringing voters to the polls. But the power of the position weakened as antipatronage laws made it harder for elected officials to hand out city jobs to people for their votes.[12] It is now largely a ceremonial party job with little power. Nevertheless, it was still a nice feather in Ortíz's cap and an embarrassment to alderman Edward Burke.

Tanya Patiño—Still a chance

A year after Aarón Ortíz's surprise victory over Daniel Burke, another young political novice decided to take on the Burke dynasty. In 2019, Tanya Patiño, 28, a civil engineer, challenged embattled Edward Burke, 76, for alderman of the Fourteenth Ward. Burke had held the aldermanic seat for fifty years. But in January 2019, federal officials charged Burke with attempted extortion. He was forced to step down as powerful chairman of the City Council's finance committee. With that dark cloud hanging over him, Patiño and other Latinos believed Burke was vulnerable and that there was a good chance to unseat him. Patiño was a lifelong resident of the ward, which is about 88 percent Latino, mainly Mexican. The ward includes parts of Archer Heights, Gage Park, Brighton Park, and Garfield Ridge. She is the daughter of Mexican immigrant parents and was involved in her community as a soccer coach. She also served as treasurer and area coordinator for state representative Aarón Ortíz, who is her partner.

Patiño argued that Burke was a machine politician who was disconnected from neighborhood residents. "Burke has gotten complacent. He never had a challenger. He just got comfortable in that position. And for him it was better to help his friends and himself versus the neighborhood," Patiño said. "You would think that our schools and parks would be top notch and they're not. . . . All his experience and connections, they've gotten us nowhere. And that's because he neglected the ward."[13] Patiño also took offense at the fact that Burke's law firm had done tax appeal work for the Trump International Hotel and Tower in Chicago, helping former president Donald Trump save millions of dollars through lowered property taxes. She questioned how an alderman can represent a largely Latino ward with compassion while working for Trump, who consistently insulted Latinos and whose immigration policies hurt Latino families.[14]

Patiño received the endorsement of Rep. Jesús García. She also received the support of some smaller unions. A third candidate, attorney Jaime Guzman, also entered the contest. "I was running on a progressive platform. I wanted to better the community by bringing better schools, better parks, and better services," said Patiño. "These are the things residents deserve, and [that] they're paying for with their taxpayer money."[15] During the campaign, Patiño alleged that Burke used city employees, many of whom were Latino, to work for him. Burke's workers put his campaign signs on people's front lawns without their permission. And his workers told some residents and business owners that if they voted for someone else, instead of Burke, they would not get services delivered to them anymore. She believed residents were afraid to vote against Burke.[16]

United States Rep. Jesús García also accused Burke of "machine-style" dirty tricks, noting that when Patiño's volunteers were in a White part of the ward they discovered a Burke pamphlet which showed Patiño's volunteers—all Black or Brown people—with the phrase, "This is what change looks like." Burke denied sending the mailer when questioned by reporters.[17] "There was racist intent behind that. What Burke was saying is that these are the Brown and Black people that are going to take over the ward," said Patiño.[18] Patiño had very little money to get her message out and relied on a series of mailers. Burke, however, had a campaign war chest of over $5 million. Burke flooded Spanish television with campaign commercials on Telemundo and Univision. The commercials emphasized the good things he did for the ward, while attacking his opponents.

In the end, Burke barely won the aldermanic race. Burke had nearly 54 percent of the vote. Tanya Patiño had nearly 30 percent and Jaime Guzman was at 16 percent.[19] Burke received 3,759 of 6,987 votes, meaning that about 270 votes would have put him in a runoff. Burke's big money, tactics, and a strong organization helped him win. Also, Patiño said, poor voter turnout hurt her; she estimated that 21,000 residents in the ward were eligible to vote. She acknowledged that although the ward is largely Mexican, a number of residents are ineligible to vote because they are undocumented. There is still the possibility that Edward Burke may be convicted for the federal charges hanging over him. "I think it's just a matter of time. I don't think he's going to complete four years," said Patiño.[20] If Burke is convicted, he would have to step down as alderman. Mayor Lori Lightfoot would then appoint an alderman to take his place. Jesús García supported Lightfoot for mayor. Plus, since Patiño came in second place in the aldermanic contest, there still is a strong chance the mayor might appoint her. "The mayor can appoint anyone, but yes, there is a chance," said Patiño.[21]

Some questioned why Jesús García continued to support new, young Latinos for elected office. A *Chicago Tribune* reporter asked if García was genuinely a progressive or the boss of a new, emerging machine; "This is no machine. I'm not a boss. We have no patronage, there is no corruption, there is no exclusion from our ranks based on gender and race. Our wins over the last few years are due to our sticking to the principles of independent progressive politics and issues," García said. "People have come around after 35 years to embracing them." [22] But outspoken and often controversial Ray Lopez, Fifteenth Ward alderman, opined that Garcia was building his own political machine. "What we're seeing is no different from the old established white machine Chuy would rail against when he was younger," Lopez said. "Democratic machine or progressive Democratic socialists, the result is the same. It's about power."[23]

Andre Vasquez—A Voice

In 2019, Andre Vasquez, a thirty-nine-year-old political newcomer, community organizer, former battle rapper, and Democratic Socialist decided to run for alderman of the city's Fortieth Ward. Most political observers did not think Vasquez had any chance of winning against the powerful, incumbent alderman Patrick O'Connor, who had been the Fortieth Ward's alderman since 1983. O'Connor was second in City Council seniority to only Alderman Edward Burke. He was Mayor Rahm Emanuel's floor leader and he assumed chairmanship of the Chicago City Council's Finance Committee after the indictment of Edward Burke forced him to relinquish the post.

The ideas of independent Vermont Senator Bernie Sanders have inspired a younger generation of activists to run for political office. Vasquez explained that he became involved in electoral politics during the 2016 presidential election as a supporter of Sanders. He was also chair of the North Side chapter of Reclaim Chicago, a progressive political action committee that attempts to limit the influence of big money in politics. He said those experiences propelled him to get involved in electoral politics. "I'm someone who was not politically involved at all. I'm just a city kid," said Vasquez. "Bernie Sanders was a person who really spoke to me because of the income inequality stances he was taking and how clear he was in his analysis. So that led me—and the fact my wife and I [are] having kids—to become more locally involved in politics."[24]

Vasquez was born in Chicago to Guatemalan immigrant parents. He attended Lane Technical College Prep High School. In his late teens and early twenties, he was a hip-hop artist, who performed under the name Prime. He attended the University of Illinois Chicago and later earned an associate degree in business administration from Kaplan University in 2014. He was a marketing manager for AT&T. Located on the city's North Side, the Fortieth Ward includes parts of Lincoln Square, West Ridge, West Andersonville, Edgewater, and Budlong Woods. Vasquez had been organizing in the ward for three years prior to his run for alderman, and many residents knew him. During the campaign, Vasquez spent a lot of time knocking on doors and talking to residents about issues that affected them. "A lot of the conversations I had were about how the city's philosophy about finance doesn't work for them. That what the city does is give all our money to corporations and megadevelopers when they should be investing in neighborhoods across the city."[25]

Vasquez's message seemed to resonate with community residents. Surprisingly, on February 26, following a five-way primary in the Fortieth Ward, Patrick O'Connor finished first with 33.3 percent of the vote compared to 20 percent for Vasquez. To avoid a runoff, O'Connor needed to get 50 percent or more of the vote. Instead, O'Connor was forced into a runoff against Vasquez in the April general election. For the first time in his thirty-six years in the City Council, O'Connor publicly stated that he could lose his aldermanic seat in the runoff election. O'Connor acknowledged that this was a change election dominated by news of the growing and ongoing City Hall corruption scandal.[26] Vasquez was endorsed by some heavy hitters including, US Rep. Jesús García, the United Working Families, the Chicago Teachers Union, and the Chicago Democratic Socialists of America—the local chapter of the national organization that supports Bernie Sanders and US Rep. Alexandria Ocasio-Cortez. "We only raised about $200,000 for the campaign. Alderman

O'Connor had a million and a half dollars. . . . They had TV ads and internet ads. We couldn't afford television ads," said Vasquez.[27]

Desperate to survive, Patrick O'Connor reached into the past and brought up the fact that Vasquez said vulgar, homophobic, misogynistic, and anti-immigrant things during his days as a battle rapper in his early twenties. The O'Conner campaign created a website to highlight Vasquez's past offensive comments. Vasquez apologized for the language he used back then as a younger man. "I think when he was talking to folks about my rap stuff, the hidden message was, 'you don't want this rap person of color from an urban environment to be the steward of this majority white, upper middle-class ward.' . . . I think it backfired. I think neighbors saw through it," said Vasquez.[28] For his part, Vasquez stressed O'Connor's long ties to the Democratic machine. Having been first elected in 1983, he was involved in the Council Wars and aligned himself with the "Vrdolyak 29" forces that opposed the policies of Harold Washington during his first three years as mayor. He was also an ally of Mayors Richard M. Daley and Rahm Emanuel.

Patrick O'Connor was endorsed by the *Chicago Tribune*. But after all the campaigning, mailers, television ads, and door-to-door conversations were over, Andre Vasquez unexpectedly beat Patrick O'Conner, with 53.93 percent of votes compared to O'Conner's 46.07 percent, a difference of more than a thousand votes. "Together, we took on the corrupt political machine at its worst and we won. . . . They outspent us seven and a half to one. Not a smart investment!" Vasquez said.[29] Interestingly, Vasquez won in a city ward that is predominately White. According to Vasquez, the Fortieth Ward is about 52 percent White, 25 percent Latino, 17 percent South Asian and Asian, and 7 percent African American. Many of the residents are middle class. The ward has many large, impressive, well-maintained homes and gardens.

As a Democratic Socialist, Vasquez favors elected public school boards, building more affordable housing, rent control, the protection of undocumented workers, and including community voices in ward-based decision-making. He is against big money in local politics and the selling or leasing of city property like Mayor Richard M. Daley did in 2008 when he leased the parking meters to a private company for 75 years for $1.15 billion—the deal was worth over three times that amount and taxpayers were enraged. "Democratic Socialism is just proving a true balance so that government provides for people and reigns in the effects of all that large money. . . . It's making sure that those who don't have the loudest voice, who don't have the most money, are being taken care of," said Vasquez. "Like in Chicago, when we look at our South and West Sides, they need more investment than the rest of the city. We need to create a fundamental change in philosophy and a change in structure of our government that makes sure that communities are the ones that are put first and foremost."[30] O'Connor never called Vasquez to congratulate him on his win. O'Connor wondered why residents were so willing to support and vote for a Socialist candidate. "Whoever thought you'd be able to say, I'm a Democratic Socialist, and people would say, That's a good thing," O'Connor told the *Sun-Times*.[31]

In addition to Vasquez's victory, three other Democratic Socialist candidates won seats in the 2019 aldermanic elections. There are now six members in Chicago's fifty-member City Council who identify themselves as Democratic Socialists. Alderman Carlos Ramirez-Rosa, Thirty-Fifth Ward, is dean of the council's Socialist Caucus, which was formed in 2019. According to Chicago's chapter of the Democratic Socialists of America (DSA), "The new socialist aldermen are going to fight for an agenda of expanding affordable housing, protecting immigrant rights, fully funding public school, expanding public services and more. That agenda will be paid for not by raising taxes on working people, but by taxing the rich."[32] According to the group there were roughly five thousand Socialist members in 2015, there are now about sixty thousand card carrying DSA members nationwide, and about thirteen hundred among three Chicago chapters.[33]

Vasquez's Guatemalan background is also noteworthy. For a long time, Guatemalans were considered a growing but "invisible community" in Chicago due to their lack of any political leaders and to a large number of undocumented individuals. It is estimated that there are over sixty-thousand Guatemalans in the Chicago area. Guatemalans quietly lived in North Side neighborhoods like Albany Park, Lincoln Square, Uptown, Edgewater, and Rodgers Park. Now, with the election of Andre Vasquez, and of Delia Ramirez (who is of Guatemalan descent) as state representative from Illinois Fourth District in 2018, the Guatemalan community has finally gained a political voice.

Joseph Berrios—"The Irish Did It"

Some Latino politicians refused to change with the times, and they see nothing wrong with machine politics. Joseph Berrios, 68, has been a fixture of Cook County politics for decades. Berrios has spent virtually his entire adult life in politics. Berrios is an old school, machine politician who came up through the regular Cook County Democratic Organization. Berrios got his start in politics while in high school as an assistant precinct captain in former alderman Thomas Keane's Thirty-First Ward. Throughout his long political career, he wholeheartedly embraced the core values of machine politics, especially the belief that the patronage system of giving high-paying government jobs to friends and family is a good thing and not something that courts and good-government types should try to get rid of. Berrios sided with the "Vrdolyak 29" and against Mayor Harold Washington during the Council Wars. Berrios does not see any differences in philosophy between politicians who call themselves "progressive," and those who are referred to as "machine politicians." "Nope. Absolutely not. What's the definition of progressive? My people instead of yours, bottom line. That's what it is," said Berrios.[34]

Berrios's parents came to Chicago from Puerto Rico and he is the oldest of seven children. Berrios came from humble beginnings. He lived in the Cabrini-Green public housing project and, later, in the Humboldt Park neighborhood. He graduated from Lane Technical College Prep High School and earned his bachelor's degree in accounting from the University of Illinois Chicago. In 1982, at age thirty, and with the backing of the Democratic machine, he was elected state representative in the Illinois General Assembly. Six years later, he was elected as a commissioner on the Cook County Board of Review, where he served for twenty-two years. In 2007, he became the first Latino chairman of the Cook County Democratic Party. And in 2010, Berrios was elected as Cook County assessor. He was also a registered Illinois state government lobbyist.

As the party's chairman, Berrios said he was able to open up the party and slate more women and minority candidates for countywide office than his predecessor.[35] Illinois state senator Omar Aquino (D-Chicago) agreed: "He doesn't get credit for the fact that when he became chairman the party changed a lot. . . . The number of Latino judges that were slated and elected to the bench in Cook County increased. It is not just Latino, there's more people of color, and women especially, that got an opportunity to be slated at the county level, not just for judges but for other positions."[36] Aquino was elected state senator of the Second District in March 2016 at the age of twenty-nine, following the resignation of Willie Delgado.

At one time, Berrios was one of the most powerful political figures in Illinois. With Berrios's assistance, his daughter, Maria Antonia Berrios, 25, and newly graduated from college, was elected as state representative of the Thirty-Ninth District of the Illinois General Assembly in 2003, and she served until 2015. But Joseph Berrios's public image began to sour. The media hammered Berrios for hiring and promoting relatives and friends while commissioner on the board of review and as Cook County assessor. The *Chicago Sun-Times* pointed out that, "Berrios won this office in 2010 on the lie that 'Joe will cut patronage positions and eliminate wasteful spending in the assessor's office.'" The *Chicago Sun-Times* then counted thirteen members of his family on county and state payrolls.[37]

Relatives of Berrios, including sisters, two sisters-in-law, a brother-in-law, and various close friends were on the Cook County assessor's payroll in jobs paying as much as $110,000 a year. Yet surprisingly, Berrios was unapologetic about patronage and hiring relatives. "They were very qualified for the jobs. They knew what the hell they were doing. They worked very hard," he said.[38] Berrios also argued that years ago, Irish machine politicians hired relatives and friends, and no one complained about it. "Yea, the Irish did it. Why shouldn't I? But the thing is, I didn't hide it."[39] Berrios sees nothing wrong with nepotism. He said people run for elected office in part to help relatives and friends. Berrios once compared his family to Democratic Party royalty. "Look at a great president we had, President Kennedy. Who'd he appoint attorney general? He appointed his brother," Berrios said. "And in government, people help many people. This is part of the process."[40]

In June 2017, the *Chicago Tribune*, later joined by *ProPublica Illinois*, began exposing how Berrios's flawed and outdated system of assessing property in Cook County resulted in punishing property tax bills for disadvantaged communities while affluent property owners hired attorneys to win assessment reductions, and downtown buildings had been systematically undervalued at the expense of small businesses in poor neighborhoods. The *Tribune's* extensive three-part investigation, "The Tax Divide," concluded that while other cities used modern technology and state-of-the-art assessment systems, Berrios used an old, outdated system that made many residential assessments inaccurate and unfair. The system favored wealthy homeowners over low-income homeowners who had fewer resources to reduce their assessments. Poor and working-class minority communities, especially African American and Latino communities, were hit the hardest.[41]

A *Chicago Tribune* editorial said that the "*Tribune* and other investigations established that Berrios' assessments system was hurting poor and minority communities. He also faced ethics questions. He hired and promoted his own family members, refused to cooperate with inquiries into his actions and routinely accepted campaign donations from lawyers seeking property valuation reductions from his office."[42] Berrios, of course, disagreed with the *Chicago Tribune*'s findings. "I inherited a system from prior assessors and you don't change these systems overnight. We went into every minority community explaining to people what their rights were and what they could do to lower their assessments," said Berrios.[43] Others, however, argued that Berrios offered a weak defense, because as a former commissioner on the Cook County Board of Review, Berrios had decades to work to make the system fair but never did.[44]

In the March 2018 Democratic primary, Fritz Kaegi, a forty-six-year-old wealthy asset manager, and newcomer to politics, challenged Berrios for the Cook County assessor's seat. Kaegi was the product of a progressive Hyde Park upbringing and put aside a lucrative investment job to make his first run for office. He pumped more than $1.3 million of his own money into his campaign. He lived in Oak Park and was a Kenwood Academy graduate with a Stanford MBA. The *Chicago Tribune* endorsed Kaegi and spoke glowingly about him. He was backed by many progressive politicians, including then county board commissioner Jesús García. For ten straight days leading up to the election, the *Chicago Tribune* ran editorials criticizing Berrios and urging voters to vote him out of office. One editorial stated, "Berrios manipulates his office to help politically connected lawyers and their clients. The tax appeal lawyers shower money on Berrios."[45] Mayor Lori Lightfoot once described Berrios as the "poster child for bad government."[46]

Challenger Fritz Kaegi trounced incumbent Joseph Berrios in the March 2018 primary by nearly 12 percentage points. Kaegi became the new Cook County assessor. After Berrios lost, he stepped down as party chairman, and Cook County board president Toni Preckwinkle took over. Berrios wondered why the *Chicago Tribune* harshly criticized him but not previous assessors—he believed he was attacked because of racism. "The *Tribune* had it in their mind that they wanted a Hispanic out of there and they did what they had to do," said Berrios.[47] In December 2019, it was announced that federal investigators were digging into Joseph Berrios's background as former Cook County assessor and his political organization. Investigators were looking to see if Berrios, as assessor, made any favorable decisions for individuals in exchange for benefits.[48] As of now, he has not been charged with any wrongdoing. The Cook

County Democratic Party gave Joseph Berrios a lifetime achievement award. "It was nice. Yes. I appreciate it," said Berrios.[49]

Rossana Rodríguez-Sanchez—Community Organizer

In 2015, political newcomer Rossana Rodríguez-Sanchez, a community activist and Columbia College Chicago student adviser, worked on the aldermanic campaign of high school teacher Tim Meegan. Meegan challenged incumbent alderman Deb Mell, Thirty-Third Ward, who was appointed in 2013 by Mayor Rahm Emanuel to fill the City Council seat left vacant that year by her powerhouse father, Alderman Richard F. Mell, who served as Thirty-Third Ward alderman for nearly forty years. Richard F. Mell was an old-guard machine politician and during the Council Wars of the mid-1980s, he was allied with the "Vrdolyak 29" who opposed Mayor Harold Washington. Prior to following in her father's aldermanic footsteps, Deb Mell represented Illinois's Fortieth District in the Illinois House of Representatives. Richard F. Mell's ward organization also helped the political career of his son-in-law, former and disgraced governor Rod Blagojevich, who is married to Mell's daughter Patti. Mell and Blagojevich later had a major falling out and refused to speak to each other.

Tim Meegan almost forced Deb Mell into a runoff election in 2015, when Mell received 50.2 percent of the votes and won the contest by seventeen votes. But after the election was over, Rodríguez-Sanchez continued organizing residents in the predominately Latino ward. "We got seventeen votes from a runoff. We didn't win. So we're going to organize ourselves and win the next one. We created the Thirty-Third Ward Working Families, and we started participating in lots of different campaigns and organizing the neighborhood around different issues," said Rodríguez-Sanchez.[50] She organized residents around issues of protections for immigrants threatened with deportation and policies aimed at gentrification, such as affordable housing and rent control to combat resident displacement.

Rodríguez-Sanchez, who was forty when she ran for office, was born and raised in Puerto Rico and moved to Chicago in 2009 after the Puerto Rican government laid off thousands of public employees amid a fiscal crisis. Her father was a community organizer. She is married and is currently raising her young son in the ethnically diverse Albany Park neighborhood. The Thirty-Third Ward includes the Northwest Side neighborhoods of Albany Park, Irving Park, Avondale, and Ravenswood Manor. Rodríguez-Sanchez found it strange that the Thirty-Third Ward is predominantly Latino but was controlled for many years by the Mell dynasty. In March 2019, Rodríguez-Sanchez, a Democratic Socialist, decided to run against Deb Mell for alderman of the Thirty-Third Ward. "I was thinking, I would love a progressive woman of color in that seat. Someone that is actually going to advocate for the people who don't have access to participation. I decided that it was important for us to fight like hell to make sure our communities are safe and healthy," said Rodríguez-Sanchez.[51]

Rodríguez-Sanchez received support, troops, and money from the Democratic Socialists of America and from various progressive unions including the powerful Chicago Teachers' Union, Service Employees International Union (SEIU) Healthcare, the National Nurses United, the Cook County Teachers Union, and the American Federation of State, County and Municipal Employees. These unions have a long track record of funding grassroots, progressive candidates and helping them win elections against machine incumbents. "That union support was crucial. And there were a lot of people in our communities that were union members that also came to work in our campaign.... We didn't take any developer money. We didn't take any corporate money," said Rodríguez-Sanchez.[52]

Rossana Rodríguez-Sanchez took the lead with 42.05 percent of the vote, followed by incumbent Deb Mell who received 41.29 percent of the vote—a difference of less than 100 votes. A third candidate, Katie Sieracke, obtained 16.66 percent of the votes. Since no candidate won more than 50 percent of the votes, Rodríguez-Sanchez and Mell headed into a runoff on April 2, 2019.[53] Rodríguez-Sanchez said there was some mudslinging in the runoff. She said Mell's camp tried to paint her as a Communist instead of a Socialist with a lot of redbaiting and fearmongering. "Look, I'm even wearing my red shoes today," she laughed. "The main thing Deb Mell tried to use against me was the message that I wanted to defund the police because I was looking at safety as a public health issue.... They also made me look a lot darker in some of their mailers."[54]

For her part, alderman Deb Mell considered herself progressive and did not like being referred to as a "machine politician" and "Daddy's little girl." Mell was the first openly gay woman to serve in the City Council and is a member of the council's LGBT Caucus. "There hasn't been a machine in the 33rd Ward for a very long time," Mell told the *Chicago Sun-Times*.[55] The *Chicago Tribune* endorsed Deb Mell and criticized Rodríguez-Sanchez because she "leans far left—she backs rent control, a federal tax on financial transactions and rein-statement of a corporate head tax."[56] The aldermanic race was too close to call, and Deb Mell asked for a partial recount. On April 18, 2019, after every last ballot was counted, Rodríguez-Sanchez beat Mell by a narrow thirteen vote margin—5,753 to 5,740. The *Chicago Sun-Times* called her a "dynasty slayer," for beating Mell. "We beat the machine. We totally did. And I think it's disin-genuous to think that there was no machine, because I believe the machine is a way of doing things," said Rodríguez-Sanchez.[57]

Rodríguez-Sanchez was incredibly proud of her win. "It is a huge accom-plishment. That family has been in that seat for forty-four years. So, for some-one who was new to electoral politics, someone that came from Puerto Rico, a community organizer, it was really a big deal. It felt really good."[58] Rodríguez-Sanchez is one of two Latina aldermen in the Chicago City Council. The other is Silvana Tabares, a former Democratic Illinois state representative, Twenty-First District, from the Southwest Side Garfield Ridge neighborhood, who was appointed in 2018 as the Twenty-Third Ward alderman by Mayor Rahm Emanuel.

Rodríguez-Sanchez is one of six Democratic Socialists in the council. As a Socialist, she firmly believes in the redistribution of wealth. "In my view, we need to make sure that we are taxing the rich, to make sure that we can pro-vide social services, to make sure that we can have healthcare for people, to make sure that the people who are creating that wealth have access to dignified lives," she said.[59] As the new alderman, Rodríguez-Sanchez said her priorities are to bring more affordable housing to the ward. Also, she said, "We have to make sure that schools are funded. We need social workers and counselors and nurses in schools. . . . We have to protect our undocumented neighbors. Where are the mental health services that mothers and children are going to need once they lose a father or a husband? How do we make sure that we're a true sanctuary city?"[60]

Delia Ramirez—Rooted and Ready

In 2018, Cynthia Soto, Democratic member of the Illinois House of Represen-tatives representing the Fourth District, announced she was retiring. Soto had served the district from 2001 to 2019. The Northwest Side's Fourth District in-cludes the Chicago neighborhoods of East Humboldt Park, Ukrainian Village, East Village, and Logan Square. Immediately, four women decided to run in the 2018 Democratic primary to fill Soto's position. The women were: Iris Millan, who worked for former First Ward alderman Proco "Joe" Moreno's ward office; Alyx Pattison and Anne Shaw, two attorneys; and Delia Ramirez, who headed a nonprofit organization in the Logan Square neighborhood. "It was all women running. All of them talked about being progressive, and it became a race of who is more progressive. . . . It was an interesting and very competitive race," said Delia Ramirez.[61]

Delia Ramirez, who was thirty-five when she ran for office, was born and raised in the Humboldt Park community. Her Guatemalan parents immigrated to Chicago in the early 1980s. "My parents were undocumented. My mother was actually pregnant with me when she was crossing the river the second time. I could have been born in Mexico. She nearly died the second time crossing the river. She was carrying me in her third trimester. . . . It is really a powerful story, but I think it speaks to the power of resilience," said Ramirez.[62] Her parents formed a homeless ministry in the Humboldt Park United Methodist Church. As a little girl, Ramirez would help her mother serve food in the soup kitchen and give food to homeless persons. Ramirez developed a passion for helping homeless and disadvantaged people. At age seventeen, Ramirez began working in a program at the ministry aimed at addressing the needs of homeless individuals. Ramirez graduated from Sabin Magnet elementary school and earned her Bachelor of Arts in justice studies from Northeastern Illinois University.

Ramirez worked for many years in various social service organizations in Humboldt Park and Logan Square. She was president of the Logan Square Neighborhood Association, executive director of the Center for Changing Lives (which helps homeless people), president of the Latin United Community Housing Association, and deputy director of the Community Renewal Society. Ramirez was initially reluctant to run for political office. She was a newcomer to politics. She did not have any name recognition. She did not have big money. And she was not sure she could win. "It meant I have to let go of my job. I have to be able to live with little or no money while I'm running for office. I have to be willing to put my reputation on the line. My reputation that I worked hard for," said Ramirez.[63] She was asked to run for political office by her neighbors and finally agreed. "I was asked to run by about thirty people who knew what I was committed to. And they said we would do all in our power to knock on doors with you. To host fundraisers for you and to make sure that people know who you are. . . . We created this true grassroots movement that activated more than seven hundred people to knock on doors," said Ramirez.[64]

Ramirez's volunteers did a lot of door knocking almost every single day. Volunteers also held more than thirty-one house parties where they collected small donations from friends and neighbors to finance her shoestring-budget campaign. "We did a lot of door knocking. My soul was 'rooted and ready,' meaning that I have deep roots in this community," said Ramirez. "I grew up in the heart of Humboldt Park and I still live there."[65] "Rooted and Ready" became the catchy slogan of her campaign. As her campaign gained momentum, others took notice. She managed to win the support of various, powerful labor unions, including SEIU Healthcare, and the Chicago Teachers Union. She was backed by Roberto Maldonado, Twenty-Sixth Ward alderman, and then Cook County commissioner Jesús García. The *Chicago Tribune* endorsed Ramirez and stated, "We're giving the nod to Ramirez, who would be a bold and aggressive voice for this district."[66]

While knocking on doors Ramirez talked to residents about public safety, building relationships with their state representative, politics, and Donald Trump. "I spend a lot of time asking them what they were looking for in the next state representative, instead of convincing them that I was what they were looking for," said Ramirez. "They said, Delia I am looking for someone who will listen, someone I can connect with. That will have an office that is actually open."[67] Ramirez considered herself a progressive politician and she liked the ideas of US senator Bernie Sanders (D-Vermont). She said, "Progressive means we are creating a space for those who have been at the margins are able to have a voice. That we're allocating and advocating resources for them, while asking those that have always had resources to step back so that others can step up."[68]

Ramirez's progressive views resonated with voters. She won the four-way race—of 14, 836 votes cast, Ramirez won 7,120, or 47.99 percent, Iris Millan won 20.73 percent, Alyx Pattison won 15.81, and Anne Shaw won 15.46. "I knocked on doors like my life depended on it. Day in and out, seven days a week, long hours. Pressing the flesh and meeting people," said Ramirez.[69] Ramirez did not have an opponent in the general election. In January 2019, she assumed office as the first Guatemalan elected to the Illinois House of Representatives. Ramirez said she was ready to advocate for Guatemalan and other working-class residents.

In May 2020, freshman state representative Delia Ramirez proposed a bill that would have canceled rent and mortgage payments for Illinoisans struggling due to the COVID-19 pandemic. But in Springfield, the bill failed to make it to the house floor for a vote. However, the *Chicago Reader* stated, "Ramirez and the coalition of housing advocates behind her were successful in pressuring state legislators to increase the amount of federal CARES Act funds the state will allocate for emergency rent and mortgage relief—almost doubling the budget from $210 million to $396 million."[70]

In this new era of Latino politics, many younger, progressive Latinos have entered politics and they view elected office as a public calling. They see themselves more as public servants than as politicians. Numerous old-guard machine politicians have been voted out of office. Other machine politicians have read the writing on the wall and have realized it is a new day. Younger elected Latinos are eagerly passing important legislation and using their political offices as a way of improving the lives of working-class people and their communities.

Epilogue

L atinos confronted major obstacles and frustrations in their attempts to acquire a political voice in Chicago politics. The long struggle was not easy; it was a rocky road. Major hurdles that hindered the political progress of early Latino immigrants to the city included the Great Depression, forced deportations, unemployment, gentrification, and low socioeconomic background. However, the biggest obstacle Latinos encountered was the indifference and neglect shown toward the Latino community for many years by Chicago's Irish-controlled political machine. As their population grew significantly over the years, Latinos—mainly Mexicans and Puerto Ricans—still lacked the political know-how and sophistication to translate their growth into an active community that could wrestle away a slice of the political pie from an entrenched and powerful Democratic political machine. For decades, Latinos were kept politically powerless and outside the halls of power, looking in.

Mayor Richard J. Daley was first elected mayor in 1955 and served until his death in 1976. For twenty-one years, Daley ran a powerful, well-oiled machine that catered to the needs of Irish and White ethnic groups but which ignored Latinos. After Daley's death, other political machine mayors, including Michael A. Bilandic and Jane M. Byrne, continued the long-established pattern of ignoring the growing Latino community and taking their vote for granted.

But through the years, Latinos became more mature and increasingly sophisticated about the intricacies of local politics. They were no longer newcomers and they were learning important lessons about how bare-knuckled politics was played in Chicago. Latinos learned how machine mayors like Richard J. Daley used the police department to infiltrate and destroy their emerging activist community groups and keep them politically disorganized. They learned firsthand the shenanigans machine politicians used to stay in power, like giving chickens and cash to people for their votes; getting elected alderman of a ward they did not live in; finding new, uncounted votes to force a runoff in a ward; and appointing handpicked, machine-backed Latinos for aldermen. Latinos learned that machine politicians would work hard to co-opt up-and-coming Latino politicians and try to silence progressive, independent Latino elected officials. Latinos learned how machine politicians would deliberately redraw state and city wards to gerrymander their communities and try to keep White politicians in power.

Latinos learned that they would have to take their fight for political empowerment to the courts—just like African Americans had done. In the early 1980s, the Mexican American Legal Defense and Educational Fund (MALDEF) filed a lawsuit alleging that several Illinois state districts were intentionally gerrymandered to dilute the voting strength of Latinos. The federal courts agreed and ordered the creation of three majority state Latino districts and one senate district. Subsequently, two Latinos were elected as state representatives and one as a state senator. Moreover, in the early 1980s, MALDEF combined with the Puerto Rican Legal Defense and Educational Fund and filed a lawsuit against the City of Chicago arguing that four majority Latino wards had been gerrymandered. The federal courts agreed with the plaintiffs and ordered that the percentage of Latino residents should be increased in four majority Latino wards and in three majority African American wards. The courts also ordered that special elections take place in those wards, and in 1986, four Latinos were elected as alderman in the City Council.

Latinos also learned how to astutely engage in political coalition building with the African American community. In 1983, Latinos backed Harold Washington for mayor even though few people believed that Washington could win the mayor's seat. After his unexpected victory, Washington supported three Latino candidates who ran for aldermen in the 1986 special elections. With Washington's backing and support, and with the combined votes of Latino and African American voters, all three candidates won office. Washington continued to endorse other Latinos for elected office many of whom also won elected office.

After Washington's death, other politicians recognized the growing influence of Latinos in local politics. In 1989, Richard M. Daley won the mayor's seat and served as mayor until 2011. Daley smartly and actively courted Latino voters. Daley supported Latinos seeking elected political office. He also appointed various Latinos to vacant aldermanic seats. But Daley was criticized by some Latino politicians for acting like a "boss" and trying to tell them how to do things. The Hispanic Democratic Organization (HDO) was actually an old-fashioned patronage army that did Mayor Daley's dirty work for many years. The HDO worked to defeat progressive Latino politicians the mayor did not like. Many Latino residents were embarrassed by the actions of the HDO and viewed the group as a step backward in the political empowerment of Latinos.

Political Progress

Since 2015, younger progressive Latino politicians have emerged on the political landscape and have been elected to various city and state offices. They seem to represent a new generation of leadership and are transforming Chicago politics. They are not old school Latino politicians beholden to the Democratic machine. Instead, they are politicians who are forward-looking and who put the community's needs above those of political party and their own personal interests. These younger Latino politicians are "more progressive. And I'm not just talking about their politics. But in terms of their skills, their knowledge, their speaking abilities, and their ability to debate," said Miguel del Valle, president of the Chicago Board of Education. "So, I think it's good. The evolution is good. It's taking us in the right direction."[1]

Latino elected officials in the city and state are becoming a powerful force to be reckoned with. A decade ago, there were twenty-three White aldermen, nineteen African American aldermen, and eight Latino aldermen. The Chicago City Council now has twelve Latino aldermen, the greatest number since the fifty-ward system was adopted in 1923. Latinos constitute 24 percent of representation on the City Council. There are twenty African Americans and eighteen White aldermen on the council.[2] Also, there are now three Latino commissioners serving on the seventeen-member Cook County Board of Commissioners. Moreover, there are now nine Latino state representatives and five Latino state senators in the Illinois General Assembly. The 2020 US Census showed that the Latino population in Chicago, Cook County, and Illinois continued to grow. Latinos now represent 29.8 percent of city, 26.2 percent of the county, and 18.2 percent of the state's population. In 2010, those numbers were 28.9 percent, 24 percent, and 15.8 percent, respectively.[3]

Latinos hope to win more elected offices now that the city's wards and the state's legislative and congressional districts have been redrawn following the 2020 US Census. The Chicago City Council approved a new ward map in May

2022. The council's Latino Caucus initially demanded that the new map include fifteen majority Latino wards—two more than now—based on the increase in Chicago's Latino population. However, the Latino Caucus eventually accepted having fourteen majority Latino wards. Moreover, in the wake of the 2020 US Census, Illinois state Democratic mapmakers created a new Third Congressional District that has about 43.7 percent voting-age Latinos. In June 2022, state Rep. Delia Ramirez won the primary for that Congressional seat with 66 percent of the vote. If she wins the general election in November 2022, she would become the first Latina from the Midwest elected to Congress.

For many years, there were very few Latino judges in Illinois. In 1994, Ruben Castillo broke barriers when he was named as the first Latino federal judge in Chicago. He served as a district judge for the Northern District of Illinois, and in 2013, he was named the first Latino chief judge. He retired in 2019. The *Chicago Tribune* stated that "Today there are approximately 40 active Latino judges in the state, serving in various parts of the court system, enough that many have recently banded together in a professional association."[4] The association is called the Illinois Latino Judges Association, and in July 2018, they held their inaugural ceremony in a downtown law office.

Latinas continue making significant inroads in the political arena by winning city and citywide offices. In 2008, history was made when Anita Alvarez was sworn in as the first Latina Cook County state's attorney. She was defeated in 2016, however, after angry African Americans refused to vote for her because she waited for almost a year to bring charges against a Chicago cop who shot teenage Laquan McDonald sixteen times. But other Latinas continue to win elected office: Latinas such as Anna M. Valencia, city clerk of Chicago; Susana A. Mendoza, Illinois comptroller; and Celina Villanueva, a former Illinois state representative, who was selected by committeemen in 2020 as the Illinois state senator (D) of the Eleventh District to replace Martin Sandoval after he stepped down as state senator when he was caught up in a bribery scandal. Edgar Gonzalez Jr., a Harvard graduate, was named to fill Villanueva's state representative vacancy.

Another Latina, Illinois state senator Iris Y. Martinez (D) of the Twentieth District made history in 2003 as the first Latina woman elected to the Illinois state senate, an office she held for seventeen years. And in November 2020, Iris Y. Martinez was elected as the first Latina Cook County circuit court clerk, an office with more than fourteen hundred employees. Martinez has promised to professionalize the clerk's office which has been criticized for its inefficiency and alleged corruption for the last twenty years under the leadership of Dorothy Brown. Upon Martinez's recommendation, members of the Cook County Democratic Party selected another Latina, Cristina Pacione-Zayas, to fill the senate seat vacated by Martinez. Pacione-Zayas earned a PhD in educational policy studies from the University of Illinois at Urbana-Champaign.

In February 2021, former Illinois House Speaker Michael Madigan handpicked a successor to the Twenty-Second House seat he stepped down from after being named in a scandal involving Commonwealth Edison putting his friends on the company's payroll in exchange for political favors. Madigan had held his legislative seat for a half-century. He picked Edward Guerra Kodatt, whose mother is from Ecuador. But three days later, Kodatt had to step down amid allegations of "questionable conduct." Madigan and four other Cook County Democratic Committee members then appointed a Latina, Angie Guerrero-Cuellar, 39, to the Twenty-Second House seat.[5] "It's important for Latina progressive women to run for office. We're the ones that are looking at politics from a very different standpoint and actually trying to change the status quo," said Illinois state senator Celina Villanueva. "I'm looking forward to this new generation of people being able to really stretch our wings and show the world what we can do."[6]

Suburbs

Many Latino residents continue to move to the suburbs surrounding Chicago. Some suburbs like Cicero, Berwyn, Aurora, Stone Park, and Waukegan have seen their Latino population, mainly Mexican, skyrocket in recent years. Between 2000 and 2010, the Latino population in Illinois grew 33 percent from 1.5 million to 2 million, and the Latino share of the population grew from 12 percent to 16 percent. Illinois's population is now over 17 percent Latino, and there are over one million eligible Latino voters in the state.[7] Most suburbs with large numbers of Mexicans are working-class suburbs with plenty of manufacturing jobs in light industries.

Despite their large numbers, for decades very few Mexicans were elected to political office in most suburbs. One major problem was that about half of adult Latinos in the metropolitan area were undocumented. Mexicans in Cicero, Illinois, made history in 2003 when they elected Republican Ramiro Gonzales, 34, as the town's first Mexican president. However, Gonzales was defeated in 2005 by Larry Dominick. Cicero has about 84,000 people of which about 89 percent are Mexican. Gonzales said he lost the election because people did not come out to vote and a sizable number are undocumented.[8] Instead of becoming naturalized US citizens—a long, complicated process—some undocumented Mexican immigrants, who suddenly find themselves unemployed, are forced to leave Illinois to seek work in other states. A 2021 Metropolitan Planning Council study found that from 2010 to 2019, about 100,000 mainly undocumented Mexican immigrants left Illinois.[9]

Some small suburbs such as Chicago Heights and Summit have managed to elect Latino mayors. In October 2004, George Pabey, a Puerto Rican man, became the first elected Latino mayor of East Chicago in Lake County, Indiana, with a population of about 28,000. But in May 2011, a judge sentenced Pabey to five years in prison for his role in a conspiracy to steal money from East Chicago. Other suburbs like Aurora, West Chicago, and Cicero have elected Latinas as Democratic state representatives to the Illinois House, and Elgin elected a Latina as a state senator. Latinos are beginning to make political gains in the suburbs as they have in the city of Chicago.

Latino Mayor of Chicago?

Many wonder when Chicago will elect its first Latino mayor. The city has elected a woman, an African American man, and an African American woman who is lesbian as mayors. It is not easy to get elected as mayor of the third-largest city in the United States. While someone's gender, race, ethnicity, or sexual orientation are important to voters, voters seem more concerned about a candidate's political message, their track record of service, and their ability to connect intimately with voters. Moreover, since the city population is about a third White, a third Latino, and a third Black, a Latino mayoral candidate will have to possess the skills to build a strong political coalition among the three major groups to achieve electoral success.

Additionally, a candidate for mayor needs an army of volunteers; strong support from big business and labor unions; and, especially important, a large, multimillion-dollar campaign war chest. In 2011, after Richard M. Daley stepped down, six candidates ran for the mayor's vacant seat including Rahm Emanuel and two Latinos, Gery Chico and Miguel del Valle. Emanuel had at his disposal a huge amount of money in his campaign war chest. He invested about fifteen million dollars and produced many television commercials to get his message out.

Del Valle's campaign, however, lacked crucial funds. He raised less than $132,000 in donations and could not afford any television advertisements. He had to rely largely on mailers to get his word out. Chico invested about $3 million in the race. Del Valle and Chico split the Latino vote. Del Valle came in third in the race with about 9 percent of the vote. Rahm Emanuel easily won the election. "It's obscene to have someone running for mayor spend $20 million. But that's what's allowed. If we had a publicly financed campaign structure, that would be different," said Miguel del Valle.[10]

In 2015, then Cook County board commissioner Jesús García ran against incumbent mayor Rahm Emanuel. García was recruited by Chicago Teachers Union (CTU) president Karen Lewis, who became ill and was forced to call off her campaign. García entered the race late, but he had the support of the CTU. Surprisingly, García won 34 percent of the vote in the February 24 primary, and Emanuel failed to win more than 50 percent, forcing a runoff election between the two on April 7. Surprisingly, most Latino politicians supported Emanuel. García believed Latino politicians were afraid to support him because "People were afraid that there would be reprisals after the election if they supported someone who could not win."[11]

García could not resurrect the African American, White, and Latino coalition that catapulted Harold Washington to the mayor's seat. It appeared many African Americans voted for Emanuel because they viewed the growing Latino community as competition—some African Americans were afraid that if Latinos are elected to higher office, African American interests would be forgotten. Also, big money loomed large in the mayoral campaign. Emanuel and his allies spent about $22.8 million in the preliminary and runoff elections. By contrast, García and his union allies spent about $4.6 million. Emanuel won the runoff election with 56 percent of the vote.[12]

After the election, Chicagoans became aware that in October 2014, an African American teenager, Laquan McDonald, holding a knife on a dark Chicago street, was walking away from police. Chicago cop Jason Van Dyke arrived on the scene and immediately shot the teenager sixteen times, killing him. It seemed Chicago police and city politicians hid the dashcam video of the shooting for over a year, until the court ordered that it be released to the public. The city agreed to pay five million dollars to McDonald's relatives even before the family filed a lawsuit. The video created outrage and anger in the African American community. Many believed Rahm Emanuel participated in hiding the video so it would not adversely affect his chances of being reelected.

African Americans felt deeply betrayed by Emanuel's actions. Had the video become public during the mayoral race, it is possible that angry African Americans would not have voted for Rahm Emanuel. Instead, perhaps they would have voted in large numbers for Jesús García, and he would have won the race. Jesús García agreed that was a possibility, "Probably. I think the video was so visceral, it was so powerful that it would have impacted the results in a dramatic way," said García.[13]

Rahm Emanuel realized that angry African Americans were not going to vote for him for reelection. Therefore, he decided not to seek reelection in 2019. Susana Mendoza, comptroller of Illinois, and Gery Chico decided to run for mayor. They joined a crowded field of fourteen candidates in the February primary. Mendoza received the highest support among Latino voters. Mendoza finished fifth in the primary election. However, neither Chico nor Mendoza advanced to the runoff for mayor. Lori Lightfoot won the runoff election against Toni Preckwinkle to become mayor.

Political Future

There are now over 62.3 million Latinos living in the United States and they make up 19 percent of the country's population. The US Census predicts that the Latino population in the United States will reach 111 million by 2060, and they will constitute 28 percent of the country's population. They are the largest ethnic group in the nation and a growing and important part of the country's future. In Chicago and Illinois, Latino residents are optimistic about their continuing quest for political empowerment. However, there is a continuing need for voter registration, education, and naturalization in the Latino community.

While Latinos in Chicago have yet to exercise their full power at the ballot box commensurate with their growing population numbers, they have made impressive gains in flexing their political muscle. They are an emerging political voice and will be key in shaping the future of Chicago politics. Alderman Rossana Rodríguez-Sanchez, Thirty-Third Ward, envisions a bright future for Latino political progress. "It's important for Latinos and Latinas to run for political office but also to stay connected to community and to activism," she said. "For Latino political progress, well, right now, it's looking great. We are only walking forward. We are not going back. We're going to fight hard."[14]

NOTES

Introduction

1. Perry R. Duis and Glen E. Holt, "Chicago's First Hispanic Alderman," *Chicago Magazine*, November 1981, 144.

2. Duis and Holt, "Chicago's First," 144.

3. Duis and Holt, "Chicago's First," 144.

4. Duis and Holt, "Chicago's First," 146.

5. "15th Ward Optimist," *Socialist* 1, no. 1 (March 8, 1914): 1.

6. Lou Ortiz, "Since 1911, Hispanics Make Headway in Chicago Politics," *Chicago Sun-Times*, August 11, 1991, 18.

7. Duis and Holt, "Chicago's First," 146.

8. Duis and Holt, "Chicago's First," 147.

9. In December 1981, Mayor Jane M. Byrne appointed Joseph José Martinez, Thirty-First Ward alderman.

10. Wilfredo Cruz, "Population Growth Fuels Latino Drive for Political Power," *Chicago Reporter*, July 1981, 1.

11. Gary Rivlin, *Fire on the Prairie: Chicago's Harold Washington and the Politics of Race* (New York: Henry Holt and Company, 1992), 349.

1. Boss Richard J. Daley and Machine Politics

1. Paul S. Taylor, *Mexican Labor in the United States* (Berkeley: University of California Press, 1932), 32.

2. Richard Santillan, "Latino Politics in the Midwestern United States: 1915–1986," in *Latinos and the Political System*, edited by F. Chris Garcia (Notre Dame, IN: University of Notre Dame Press, 1988), 103.

3. Santillan, "Latino Politics," 104.

4. Abraham Hoffman, *Unwanted Mexican Americans in the Great Depression: Repatriation Pressures, 1929–1939* (Tucson: The University of Arizona Press, 1974).

5. Louise Año Nuevo-Kerr, "The Chicano Experience in Chicago, 1920–1970" (PhD diss., University of Illinois Chicago, 1976), 19.

6. Santillan, "Latino Politics," 104.

7. Elena Padilla, "Puerto Rican Immigrants in New York and Chicago: A Study in Comparative Assimilation" (MA thesis, University of Chicago, June 1947), 49.

8. Edwin Maldonado, "Contract Labor and the Origins of Puerto Rican Communities," in *Forging a Community: The Latino Experience in Northwest Indiana, 1919–1975,* edited by James B. Lane and Edward J. Escobar (Chicago: Cattails Press, 1987), 206.

9. Wilfredo Cruz, *City of Dreams: Latino Immigration to Chicago* (Lanham, MD: University Press of America, 2007), 82.

10. David A. Badillo, "From La Lucha to Latino," in *La Causa: Civil Rights, Social Justice and the Struggle for Equality in the Midwest,* ed. Gilberto Cárdenas (Houston, TX: Arte Público Press, 2004), 37.

11. Cruz, *City of Dreams,* 79.

12. Elly Fishman, "José López's Last Stand," *Chicago Magazine,* October 21, 2014, 2.

13. Richard Allen Morton, *Roger C. Sullivan and the Making of the Chicago Democratic Machine, 1881–1908* (Jefferson, NC: McFarland, 2016).

14. Dennis R. Judd and Annika M. Hinze, *City Politics: The Political Economy of Urban America* (New York: Routledge, 2019).

15. Paul M. Green, "Mayor Richard J. Daley and the Politics of Good Government," in *The Mayors: The Chicago Political Tradition,* ed. Paul M. Green and Melvin G. Holli (Carbondale: Southern Illinois University Press, 2013), 145.

16. Green, "Mayor Richard J. Daley," 144.

17. Judd and Hinze, *City Politics.*

18. Adam Cohen and Elizabeth Taylor, *American Pharaoh: Mayor Richard J. Daley; His Battle for Chicago and the Nation* (New York: Back Bay Books, 2000), 155.

19. William J. Grimshaw, *Bitter Fruit: Black Politics and the Chicago Machine, 1931–1991* (Chicago: The University of Chicago Press, 1992), 185.

20. Steven P. Erie, *Rainbow's End: Irish-Americans and the Dilemmas of Urban Machine Politics, 1840–1985* (Berkeley: University of California Press, 1988), 10.

21. Erie, *Rainbow's End,* 10.

22. Carlos Herñandez-Gómez, "Population Soars, but Political Power Lags," *Chicago Reporter,* September 1, 2001, 1.

23. Mike Amezcua, "A Machine in the Barrio: Chicago's Conservative Colonia and the Remaking of Latino Politics in the 1960s and 1970s." *Sixties* 12, no. 1 (2019): 5.

24. Amezcua, "Chicago's Conservative Colonia," 5.

25. Cohen and Taylor, *American Pharaoh,* 157.

26. Grimshaw, *Bitter Fruit,* 185.

27. William J. Grimshaw, "The Daley Legacy," in *After Daley: Chicago Politics in*

Transition, ed. Samuel K. Gove and Louis H. Masotti (Urbana: University of Illinois Press, 1982), 77.

28. Luis M. Corral, "Hernandez Led way for Hispanic Politicians Here," *Chicago Sun-Times*, September 20, 1991, 24.

29. "Amigos for Daley Speech," March 26, 1975, McCormick Place, Chicago IL, University of Illinois at Chicago, Richard J. Daley Library, folder 7, box SIss1B1, 1.

30. "Amigos for Daley," 2.

31. Jaime Dominguez, "Latinos in Chicago: A Strategy Towards Political Empowerment (1975–2003)" (PhD diss., University of Illinois at Chicago, 2007), 88.

32. Luis M. Salces and Peter W. Colby, "Spanish-American Politics in Chicago," in *Latinos and the Political System*, ed. F. Chris Garcia (Notre Dame, IN: University of Notre Dame Press, 1988), 195.

33. Amezcua, "Chicago's Conservative Colonia," 17.

34. Patricia Mendoza, "Latinos and the Growth of Political Empowerment in Illinois," in *La Causa: Civil Rights, Social Justice and the Struggle for Equality in the Midwest*, ed. Gilberto Cárdenas (Houston, TX: Arte Público Press, 2004), 20.

35. Melita Maria Garza, "In World of Politics, Hispanics Feel Left Out," *Chicago Tribune*, October 21, 1992, 4.

36. David K. Fremon, *Chicago Politics Ward by Ward* (Bloomington: Indiana University Press, 1988), 203.

37. Fremon, *Chicago Politics*, 203.

38. Mike Royko, *Boss: Richard J. Daley of Chicago* (New York: Plume Book, 1988), 152.

39. Author interview with Joseph Berrios, March 1, 2019, Chicago.

40. Author interview with Miguel del Valle, March 15, 2019, Chicago.

41. Terry Nichols Clark, "The Irish Ethic and the Spirit of Patronage," *Ethnicity* 2, no. 4 (1975): 338.

42. Cruz, *City of Dreams*, 119.

43. Len O'Connor, *Clout: Mayor Daley and His City* (Chicago: Contemporary Books, 1975), 252.

44. Berrios interview.

45. Cruz, *City of Dreams*, 57.

46. Robert Davis, "Hispanics Ask Apology," *Chicago Tribune*, January 13, 1983, 2.

47. Milton L. Rakove, *We Don't Want Nobody Nobody Sent: An Oral History of the Daley Years* (Bloomington: Indiana University Press, 1979), 128.

48. Ben Joravsky, "Pilsen Street Hustler Takes on Old Guard at City Hall," *Chicago Reporter*, November 1984, 3.

49. Cruz, *City of Dreams*, 23.

50. Cruz, *City of Dreams*, 24.

51. John Adam Moreau, "Young Lords Emulate the Black Panthers," *Chicago Sun-Times*, June 5, 1969, 14.

52. Ron Grossman, "How a Street Gang Turned to Community Activism," *Chicago Tribune*, July 8, 2018, 21.

53. Cruz, "Population Growth," 1.

54. Roger Biles, *Richard J. Daley: Politics, Race, and the Governing of Chicago* (DeKalb: Northern Illinois University Press, 1995), 122.

55. "Crowd Burns 2 Police Cars," *Chicago Sun-Times*, June 13, 1966, 1.

56. Chicago Commission on Human Relations, "The Puerto Rican Residents of Chicago," 1966.

57. Royko, *Boss*, 152.

58. "San Juan Theater Speech," Not dated. Chicago, University of Illinois at Chicago, Richard J. Daley Library, folder 7, box SIss1B1, 1.

59. Amezcua, "Chicago's Conservative Colonia," 12.

60. Biles, *Richard J. Daley*, 125.

61. Biles, *Richard J. Daley*, 126.

62. Cruz, *City of Dreams*, 84.

63. Cruz, *City of Dreams*, 84.

64. Tom Gibbons and Adrienne Drell, "Hispanics Win 'Red Squad' Suit," *Chicago Sun-Times*, June 30, 1984, 6.

65. Cohen and Taylor, *American Pharaoh*, 558.

66. Cohen and Taylor, *American Pharaoh*, 558.

2. Michael A. Bilandic and Jane M. Byrne

1. Roger Biles, *Richard J. Daley: Politics, Race, and the Governing of Chicago* (DeKalb: Northern Illinois University Press, 1995) 232.

2. Kathleen A. Kemp and Robert L. Lineberry, "The Last of the Great Urban Machines and the Last of the Great Urban Mayors? Chicago Politics, 1955–1977," in *After Daley: Chicago Politics in Transition*, ed. Samuel K. Gove and Louis H. Masotti (Urbana: University of Illinois Press, 1982), 19.

3. Paul M. Green, "Michael A. Bilandic: The Last of the Machine Regulars." In *The Mayors: The Chicago Political Tradition*, ed. Paul M. Green and Melvin G. Holli (Carbondale: Southern Illinois University Press, 2013), 160.

4. Joanne Belenchia, "Latinos and Chicago Politics," in *After Daley: Chicago Politics in Transition*, ed. Samuel K. Gove and Louis H. Masotti (Urbana: University of Illinois Press, 1982), 118.

5. Author interview with Ben Joravsky, February 2, 2019, Chicago.

6. Green, "Michael A. Bilandic," 162.

7. Biles, *Richard J. Daley*, 234.

8. Michael B. Preston, "Black Politics in the Post-Daley Era," in *After Daley: Chicago Politics in Transition*, ed. Samuel K. Gove and Louis H. Masotti (Urbana: University of Illinois Press, 1982), 106.

9. Eugene Kennedy, "Hard Times in Chicago," *New York Times Magazine*, March 19, 1980, 23.

10. Bill Granger and Lori Granger, *Fighting Jane* (New York: The Dial Press, 1980), 193.

11. Declaration of Candidacy of Jane Byrne. Jane Byrne for Mayor. Monadnock Building, 53 W. Jackson Blvd., Room 1062, Chicago. April 24, 1978, 1.

12. Paul Kleppner, *Chicago Divided: The Making of a Black Mayor* (DeKalb: Northern Illinois University Press, 1985), 115.

13. Kathleen Whalen FitzGerald, *Brass: Jane Byrne and the Pursuit of Power* (Chicago: Contemporary Books, 1981), 202.

14. Granger and Granger, *Fighting Jane*, 19.

15. Melvin G. Holli, "Jane M. Byrne: To Think the Unthinkable and Do the Undoable," in *The Mayors: The Chicago Political Tradition*, ed. Paul M. Green and Melvin G. Holli (Carbondale: Southern Illinois University Press, 2013), 169.

16. Jane Byrne, *My Chicago* (New York: W. W. Norton, 1992), 330.

17. Holli, "Jane M. Byrne," 171.

18. Holli, "Jane M. Byrne," 173.

19. FitzGerald, *Brass*, 194.

20. FitzGerald, *Brass*, 205.

21. FitzGerald, *Brass*, 205.

22. FitzGerald, *Brass*, 206.

23. FitzGerald, *Brass*, 206.

24. Kennedy, "Hard Times," 76.

25. Wilfredo Cruz, *City of Dreams: Latino Immigration to Chicago* (Lanham, MD: University Press of America, 2007), 85.

26. William J. Grimshaw, "Harold Washington: The Enigma of the Black Political Tradition," in *The Mayors: The Chicago Political Tradition*, ed. Paul M. Green and Melvin G. Holli (Carbondale: Southern Illinois University Press, 2013), 192.

27. Holli, "Jane M. Byrne," 76.

28. Belenchia, "Latinos," 141.

29. Granger and Granger, *Fighting Jane*, 195.

30. Granger and Granger, *Fighting Jane*, 223.

31. Granger and Granger, *Fighting Jane*, 232.

32. Cruz, "Population Growth," 1.

33. Cruz, "Population Growth," 2.

34. Cruz, "Population Growth," 2.

35. Wilfredo Cruz, "Joseph José Martinez," *Chicago Reporter*, January 1982, 8.

36. Cruz, *City of Dreams,* 119.

37. Cruz, "Population Growth," 5.

38. David K. Fremon, *Chicago Politics Ward by Ward* (Bloomington: Indiana University Press, 1988), 207.

39. Patricia Mendoza, "Latinos and the Growth of Political Empowerment in Illinois," in *La Causa: Civil Rights, Social Justice and the Struggle for Equality in the Midwest,* ed. Gilberto Cárdenas (Houston: Arte Público Press, 2004), 22.

40. Mendoza, "Latinos," 23.

41. Author interview with Virginia Martinez, August 31, 2017, Chicago.

42. Mendoza, "Latinos," 23.

43. Martinez interview.

44. Cruz, *City of Dreams,* 120.

45. Mendoza, "Latinos," 21.

46. Mendoza, "Latinos," 23.

47. Martinez Interview.

48. David K. Fremon, "Chicago's Spanish-American Politics in the '80s," *Illinois Issues,* January 1990, 20.

49. Alton Miller, *Harold Washington: The Mayor, The Man* (Chicago: Bonus Books, 1989), 257.

50. Mendoza, "Latinos," 22.

51. Martinez interview.

52. Wilfredo Cruz, "Minority Leaders Charge Police with Disorderly Conduct." *Chicago Reporter,* October 1982, 1.

53. Police Accountability Task Force. "Restoring Trust Between the Chicago Police and the Communities They Serve," April 2016, 34.

54. Melvin G. Holli and Paul M. Green, *Bashing Chicago Traditions Traditions: Harold Washington's Last Campaign, Chicago, 1987* (Grand Rapids, MI: William B. Eerdmans, 1989), 146.

55. Diana Novak Jones, "Jane Byrne Interchange Dedicated," *Chicago Sun-Times,* August 30, 2014, 6.

3. Harold Washington and Reform

1. William J. Grimshaw, "Harold Washington: The Enigma of the Black Political Tradition." In *The Mayors: The Chicago Political Tradition,* ed. Paul M. Green and Melvin G. Holli (Carbondale: Southern Illinois University Press), 188.

2. William J. Grimshaw, *Bitter Fruit: Black Politics and the Chicago Machine, 1931–1991* (Chicago: The University of Chicago Press, 1992), 5.

3. Don Rose, "The Rise of Independent Black Political Power in Chicago," in *The Chicago Freedom Movement: Martin Luther King Jr. and Civil Rights Activism in the North*, ed. Mary Lou Finley et al. (Lexington: University Press of Kentucky, 2015), 263.

4. Rose, "The Rise," 263.

5. Grimshaw, *Bitter Fruit*, 94.

6. Rose, "The Rise," 267.

7. Grimshaw, *Bitter Fruit*, 94.

8. Melvin G. Holli and Paul M. Green, *Bashing Chicago Traditions: Harold Washington's Last Campaign, Chicago, 1987* (Grand Rapids, MI: William B. Eerdmans, 1989), 183.

9. Holli and Green, *Bashing Chicago*, 183.

10. Paul Kleppner, *Chicago Divided: The Making of a Black Mayor* (DeKalb: Northern Illinois University Press, 1985), 153.

11. Teresa Córdova, "Harold Washington and the Rise of Latino Electoral Politics in Chicago, 1982–1987," in *Chicano Politics and Society in the Late Twentieth Century*, ed. David Montejano (Austin: University of Texas Press, 1999), 31.

12. Wilfredo Cruz, *City of Dreams: Latino Immigration to Chicago* (Lanham, MD: University Press of America, 2007), 58.

13. Manuel Galvan, "Lozano's Slaying Called Political Assassination," *Chicago Tribune*, June 10, 1983, 2.

14. *Rudy Lozano, His Life, His People* (Chicago: Taller de Estudios Comunitarios, 1984).

15. Cruz, *City of Dreams*, 58.

16. Kleppner, *Chicago Divided*, 161.

17. María de los Angeles Torres, "The Commission on Latino Affairs," in *Harold Washington and the Neighborhoods: Progressive City Government in Chicago, 1983–1987*, ed. Pierre Clavel and Wim Wiewel (New Brunswick, NJ: Rutgers University Press, 1991), 171.

18. Kleppner, *Chicago Divided*, 208.

19. Torres, "The Commission," 172.

20. Manuel Galvan, "Hispanic Voting Bloc Goes Strong for Washington," *Chicago Tribune*, June 10, 1983, 4.

21. Gary Rivlin, *Fire on the Prairie: Chicago's Harold Washington and the Politics of Race* (New York: Henry Holt, 1992), 352.

22. Ben Joravsky, "Mayor Slow to Fill Top City Jobs," *Chicago Reporter*, August 1, 1984. 1.

23. Alton Miller, *Harold Washington: The Mayor, The Man* (Chicago: Bonus Books, 1989), 156.

24. Cruz, *City of Dreams*, 59.

25. Rivlin, *Fire on the Prairie,* 352.

26. Holli and Green, *Bashing,* 138.

27. Ben Joravsky and Jorge Casuso, "Hispanic Vote Emerges as New Battlefront in Council Wars," *Chicago Reporter,* September 1984, 8.

28. Rivlin, *Fire on the Prairie,* 354.

29. Rivlin, *Fire on the Prairie,* 354.

30. Fremon, *Chicago Politics,* 166.

31. Rivlin, *Fire on the Prairie,* 356.

32. Jorge Casuso and Ben Joravsky, "El Gallito," *Chicago Tribune,* June 4, 1989, 2.

33. Luis Gutiérrez, *Still Dreaming: My Journey from the Barrio to Capitol Hill* (New York: W. W. Norton, 2013), 223.

34. Grimshaw, *Bitter Fruit,* 182.

35. Fremon, *Chicago Politics,* 167.

36. Manuel Galvan and Mark Eissman, "Hispanics Rejoice," *Chicago Tribune,* March 26, 1986, 1.

37. Gutiérrez, *Still Dreaming,* 236.

38. Gutiérrez, *Still Dreaming,* 237.

39. Gutiérrez, *Still Dreaming,* 238.

40. Cruz, *City of Dreams,* 121.

41. Cruz, *City of Dreams,* 60.

42. Author interview with Jesús García, June 21, 2018, Chicago.

43. Rivlin, *Fire on the Prairie,* 352.

44. Rivlin, *Fire on the Prairie,* 352.

45. Rivlin, *Fire on the Prairie,* 358.

46. Cruz, *City of Dreams,* 178.

47. Miller, *Harold Washington,* 172.

48. Miller, *Harold Washington,* 173.

49. Cruz, *City of Dreams,* 178.

50. Cruz, *City of Dreams,* 178.

51. García interview.

52. García interview.

53. Holli and Green, *Bashing,* 19.

54. Holli and Green, *Bashing,* 21.

55. Holli and Green, *Bashing,* 22.

56. Holli and Green, *Bashing,* 23.

57. Holli and Green, *Bashing,* 111.

58. Holli and Green, *Bashing,* 112.

4. Eugene Sawyer and Richard M. Daley

1. Monroe Anderson, "The Sawyer Saga: A Journalist, Who Just Happened to Be the Mayor's Press Secretary, Speaks." In *The Mayors: The Chicago Political Tradition,* Paul M. Green and Melvin G. Holli, eds. (Carbondale: Southern Illinois University Press, 2013), 211.

2. Jon Yates and Tara Malone, "Eugene Sawyer," *Chicago Tribune,* January 21, 2008, 2.

3. Anderson, "The Sawyer Saga," 212.

4. William J. Grimshaw, *Bitter Fruit: Black Politics and the Chicago Machine, 1931–1991* (Chicago: The University of Chicago Press, 1992), 200.

5. Anderson, "The Sawyer Saga," 212.

6. Grimshaw, *Bitter Fruit,* 201.

7. Cheryl Devall, "Coalition Urged to Challenge Mayor in 1989," *Chicago Tribune,* January 25, 1988, 1.

8. Devall, "Coalition," 1.

9. R. Bruce Dold, "Not His 'Hispanic Agenda,'" *Chicago Tribune,* February 17, 1989, 1.

10. Dold, "Not His," 1.

11. Jean Latz Griffin, "Study Asks Hispanic Medical Chief," *Chicago Tribune,* December 2, 1988, 1.

12. Griffin, "Study," 2.

13. Griffin, "Study," 2.

14. Jorge Casuso and Ben Joravsky, "What Makes Luis Run?" *Chicago Tribune Magazine,* June 4, 1989, 20.

15. Wilfredo Cruz, *City of Dreams: Latino Immigration to Chicago* (Lanham, MD: University Press of America, 2007), 122.

16. Paul M. Green, "Richard M. Daley and the Politics of Addition," in Paul M. Green and Melvin G. Holli, eds., *The Mayors: The Chicago Political Tradition* (Carbondale: Southern Illinois University Press, 2013), 226.

17. Jim Merriner, "Daley Got 71% of Hispanic Vote," *Chicago Sun-Times,* March 13, 1989, 5.

18. Steve Neal, "Daley Still Popular Among Hispanics," *Chicago Sun-Times,* February 4, 1991, 25.

19. Green, "Richard M. Daley," 223.

20. Grimshaw, *Bitter Fruit,* 206.

21. Casuso and Joravsky, "El Gallito," 2.

22. Casuso and Joravsky, "El Gallito," 2.

23. John Kass, "Gutiérrez's Tax Bill," *Chicago Tribune,* August 2, 1998, 3.

24. Green, "Richard M. Daley," 214.

25. Jennifer Juarez Robles, "Mayor Daley Quiet on Racial Issues," *Chicago Reporter*, July 1, 1989, 3.

26. Constanza Montana, "Daley Uses Deft Touch," *Chicago Tribune*, June 4, 1989, 2.

27. Sharman Stein, "Rodriguez Chosen for Top Police Post," *Chicago Tribune*, April 13, 1992, 1.

28. Steve Mills and Andrew Martin, "Rodriguez's Friendship with Felon," *Chicago Tribune*, November 14, 1997, 1.

29. Thomas J. Gradel and Dick Simpson, *Corrupt Illinois: Patronage, Cronyism, and Criminality* (Chicago: University of Illinois Press, 2015), 136.

30. Gradel and Simpson, *Corrupt Illinois*, 137.

31. Cruz, *City of Dreams*, 122.

32. Cruz, *City of Dreams*, 122.

33. Costas Spirou and Dennis R. Judd, *Building the City of Spectacle: Mayor Richard M. Daley and the Remaking of Chicago* (Ithaca: Cornell University Press, 2016), 134.

34. Cruz, *City of Dreams*, 123.

35. Cruz, *City of Dreams*, 124.

36. Cruz, *City of Dreams*, 124.

37. Wilfredo Cruz, "All Politics Is Local," *In These Times*, April 14, 1997, 14.

38. Cruz, *City of Dreams*, 124.

39. Cruz, *City of Dreams*, 215.

40. Cruz, *City of Dreams*, 178.

41. "Schools in Chicago Are Called the Worst," *New York Times*, November 8, 1987, 4.

42. Lourdes Monteagudo, "One Can Make a Difference," *Chicago Tribune*, September 2, 1990, 3.

43. Cruz, *City of Dreams*, 50.

44. Fran Spielman, "Chico ad," *Chicago Sun-Times*, November 8, 2018, 3.

45. Cruz, *City of Dreams*, 50.

46. Virginia Valdez, "Chicago Public School's Efforts to Relieve Overcrowding," *Mexican American Legal Defense and Educational Fund*, April 2000, 2.

47. "Rebuilding Our Schools," *The Neighborhood Capital Budget Group*, November 1999, 9.

48. Spielman, "Chico Ad," 3.

49. Ray Quintanilla, "Hispanic Area May Get 2 High Schools," *Chicago Tribune*, August 21, 2001, 1.

50. Tim Novak and Steve Warmbir, "You Just Sit on the Job," *Chicago Sun-Times*, January 23, 2004, 3.

51. Gradel and Simpson, *Corrupt Illinois*, 75.

52. Steve Warmbir and Tim Novack, "Members of Hispanic Organization Run Program," *Chicago Sun-Times*, February 6, 2004, 1.

53. Gradel and Simpson, *Corrupt Illinois*, 75.

54. Dan Mihalopoulos and James Kimberly, "Inside Daley's Machine," *Chicago Tribune*, June 21, 2006, 1.

55. Dan Mihalopoulos and Rudolph Bush, "Sorich Gets 46 Months," *Chicago Tribune*, November 21, 2006, 1.

56. Keith Koeneman, *First Son Son: The Biography of Richard M. Daley* (Chicago: The University of Chicago Press, 2013), 252.

57. Jeff Coen and Dan Mihalopoulos, "Ex-Daley Aide Sanchez Guilty," *Chicago Tribune*, March 23, 2009, 1.

58. Laurie Cohen, Jorge Luis Mota, and Andrew Martin, "Hispanic Organization Builds Machine-Like Power in City," *Chicago Tribune*, October 31, 2002, 1.

59. Cohen, Mota, and Martin, "Hispanic Organization," 1.

60. Cohen, Mota, and Martin, "Hispanic Organization," 1.

61. Spirou and Judd, *Building the City*, 8.

62. Cohen, Mota, and Martin, "Hispanic Organization," 2.

63. Cruz, *City of Dreams*, 61.

64. Cruz, *City of Dreams*, 61.

65. Cruz, *City of Dreams*, 61.

66. Cruz, *City of Dreams*, 62.

67. Cruz, *City of Dreams*, 62.

68. Cruz, *City of Dreams*, 62.

69. Cruz, *City of Dreams*, 64.

70. Author interview with Ben Joravsky, February 2, 2019, Chicago.

71. Todd Lighty and Dan Mihalopoulos, "Once Powerful Hispanic Organization Gone," *Chicago Tribune*, July 3, 2008, 1.

72. Annie Sweeney, "Ex-Streets and San Boss Gets 2½ Years," *Chicago Tribune*, February 3, 2011, 2.

73. Coen and Mihalopoulos, "Ex-Daley aide," 6.

74. Coen and Mihalopoulos, "Ex-Daley aide," 6.

75. Coen and Mihalopoulos, "Ex-Daley aide," 6.

76. Cruz, *City of Dreams*, 125.

77. William Neikirk, "Gutiérrez Unhappy with 'Old Boss' Daley," *Chicago Tribune*, March 12, 2000, 10.

78. Lynn Sweet, "Mayor Pledges Support for Congressman's Re-election," *Chicago Tribune*, June 26, 2001, 35.

79. Spirou and Judd, *Building the City*, 175.

80. "Daley's Decades," *Chicago Tribune*, April 20, 2011, 13.

81. Spirou and Judd, *Building the City*, 174.

82. Bob Secter, "Daley Won't Run for Record Seventh Election" *Chicago Tribune*, September 8, 2010, 1.

5. Fall from Grace

1. Hannah Alani, "Chicago Is the Most Corrupt City," *Block Club Chicago*, February 18, 2020, 1.

2. Alani, "Chicago," 1.

3. Carlos Herñandez-Gómez, "Medrano Takes Blame for 'Mistake,'" *Chicago Reporter*, January 1, 2001, 1.

4. Herñandez-Gómez, "Medrano," 1.

5. Fran Spielman, "Medrano Back Where He Started," *Chicago Sun-Times*, June 28, 2012, 3.

6. Herñandez-Gómez, "Medrano," 2.

7. Thomas J. Gradel and Dick Simpson, *Corrupt Illinois: Patronage, Cronyism, and Criminality* (Chicago: University of Illinois Press, 2015), 63.

8. Jon Seidel, "Ambrosio Medrano Released," *Chicago Sun-Times*, May 15, 2020, 3.

9. Seidel, "Ambrosio Medrano," 3.

10. Wilfredo Cruz, "Joseph José Martinez," *Chicago Reporter*, January 1982, 8.

11. Cruz, "Joseph José Martinez," 8.

12. "Former Chicago Alderman Pleads Guilty," *Associated Press*, January 24, 1997, 1.

13. Charles Sheehan, "Disbarred Ex-alderman Can Be Reinstated," *Chicago Tribune*, May 19, 2006, 2.

14. Matt O'Connor, "Ghost Worker Sentenced to 5 Months," *Chicago Tribune*, January 29, 1998, 1.

15. O'Connor, "Ghost Worker," 1.

16. Sheehan, "Disbarred," 2.

17. Matt O'Connor and Gary Washburn, "Time to Belly Up," *Chicago Tribune*, May 4, 1999, 1.

18. O'Connor and Washburn, "Time to Belly Up," 1.

19. Carlos Herñandez-Gómez, "Minorities Go To Trial Faster," *Chicago Reporter*, January 1, 2001, 1.

20. Fran Spielman, "Misery Loves Company?" *Chicago Sun-Times*, February 13, 2006, 5.

21. Spielman, "Misery Loves Company?" 5.

22. Fran Spielman, "Hispanic Leaders Rally behind Santos," *Chicago Sun-Times*, November 6, 1991, 3.

23. O'Connor and Washburn, "Time to Belly Up," 1.

24. Marja Mills, "Miriam Santos Gets 40 Months," *Chicago Tribune*, July 27, 1999, 1.

25. Mills, "Miriam Santos," 1.

26. "City Treasurer Resigns," *Associated Press*, October 28, 2000, 1.

27. Mike Robinson, "Chicago City Treasurer Pleads Guilty," *Associated Press*, October 28, 2000, 1.

28. "Rey Colón, Candidate for 35th Ward Alderman," *ABC 7 Online Candidates Forum*, February 1, 2015.

29. Hal Dardick, "Alderman, 35th, Charged with DUI," *Chicago Tribune*, July 29, 2014, 3.

30. Gwynedd Stuart, "Can a 26-Year-Old Beat Rey Colón? *Chicago Reader*, December 30, 2014, 3.

31. Darryl Holliday, "Carlos Ramirez-Rosa," *DNAinfo*, February 24, 2015, 1.

32. Stuart, "Can a 26-Year-Old," 3.

33. Steve Schmadeke, "Ex-commissioner Gets 11 Years," *Chicago Tribune*, February 19, 2014, 7.

34. Ben Jorvasky, "What's He Up To?" *Chicago Reader*, March 27, 2003, 3.

35. Jorvasky, "What's He Up To?" 3.

36. Schmadeke, "Ex-commissioner," 7.

37. "Moreno Sentenced to 11 Years," *U.S. Attorney's Office*, February 19. 2014, 1.

38. Schmadeke, "Ex-commissioner," 7.

39. Jonathan Bilyk, "Ex-wife Sues Lawyers," *Cook County Record*, February 9, 2016, 1.

40. Rosemary Sobol and John Byrne, "Moreno Flashed City Council Badge," *Chicago Tribune*, June 20, 2018, 3.

41. Sobol and Byrne, "Moreno," 3.

42. "Endorsements: 13 Candidates for City Council," *Chicago Sun-Times*, February 6, 2019, 23.

43. Andy Grimm and Matthew Hendrickson, "Alderman Charged," *Chicago Sun-Times*, May 16, 2019, 2.

44. Jason Meisner, "Charged with Filing False Report," *Chicago Tribune*, May 17, 2019, 7.

45. Megan Crepeau, "Moreno Charged with Car Insurance Fraud," *Chicago Tribune*, May 16, 2019, 7.

46. Sam Charles, "Ex-Ald. Proco 'Joe' Moreno Charged With DUI in Crash," *Chicago Sun-Times*, December 29, 2020, 1.

47. Rosemary Sobol, "Munoz Approved to Seek Counseling," *Chicago Tribune*, January 24, 2019, 5.

48. Author interview with Ricardo Muñoz, June 7, 2018, Chicago.

49. Muñoz interview.

50. Rosemary Sobol, "Munoz, Wife to Reconcile," *Chicago Tribune*, February 28, 2019, 5.

51. Sobol, "Munoz approved," 5.

52. Mitch Dudek, "Wife Flips Off Ald. Munoz," *Chicago Sun-Times*, March 21, 2019, 4.

53. Andy Grimm, "She Fears Husband's 'Connections' with Gangs," *Chicago Sun-Times*, January 5, 2019, 4.

54. Dudek, "Wife Flips Off," 4.

55. Mitch Dudek, "Ald. Munoz Accused of Raiding Progressive Caucus Fund," *Chicago Sun-Times*, April 4, 2019, 5.

56. Jason Meisner, "Ex-state Rep. Arroyo Likely to Plead Guilty," *Chicago Tribune*, January 18, 2020, 1.

57. Meisner, "Ex-state Rep. Arroyo," 2.

58. Jason Meisner, "Arroyo Pleads Not Guilty," *Chicago Tribune*, February 5, 2020, 8.

59. Meisner, "Arroyo Pleads," 8.

60. Jon Seidel, "Lawmaker Link Hit with Federal Tax Charge," *Chicago Sun-Times*, August 14, 2020, 15.

61. Mark Brown, "Luis Arroyo," *Chicago Sun-Times*, November 3, 2019, 2.

62. Dan Petrella, "Pick by Cook Dems," *Chicago Tribune*, November 17, 2019, 1.

63. Rich Miller, "Tumultuous Day in Springfield," *Chicago Sun-Times*, November 3, 2019, 34.

64. David Heinzmann, "Feds Eye Who's Who in Sandoval Case," *Chicago Tribune*, October 13, 2019, 1.

65. Jason Meisner, "Political Operative Pleads Not Guilty," *Chicago Tribune*, March 11, 2020, 4.

66. Jason Meisner and Megan Crepeau, "Guilty Plea Bares Sandoval's Greed," *Chicago Tribune*, January 29, 2020, 1.

67. Meisner and Crepeau. "Guilty Plea," 5.

68. Fran Spielman, "Medrano Back to Where He Started," *Chicago Sun-Times*, June 28, 2012, 3.

69. Lolly Bowean, "25th Ward Candidates Came to Talk Housing," *Chicago Tribune*, January 26, 2019, 3.

70. Fran Spielman, "Burke Loses Party Post," *Chicago Sun-Times*, March 19, 2020, 6.

71. John Byrne, "FBI Probes Corruption," *Chicago Tribune*, February 4, 2019, 1.

72. Wilfredo Cruz, "From Blue Jeans to Pinstripes," *Illinois Issues*, December 1993, 20.

73. Dan Mihalopoulos, "Taxpayers Paying For UNO Schools," *Chicago Sun-Times*, December 4, 2016, 1.

74. "As the Feds Narrow Their Target," *Chicago Tribune*, July 28, 2019, 13.

75. Gregory Pratt, "Pension Remains Despite Scandal," *Chicago Tribune*, September 16, 2019, 1.

76. Hal Dardick, Jason Meisner, and David Heinzmann, "Ald. Daniel Solis," *Chicago Tribune*, January 29, 2019, 1.

77. Jason Meisner, Jeff Cohen, Stacy St. Clair, and Christy Gutowski, "Bombshell Filing," *Chicago Tribune*, March 14, 2019, 1.

78. Meisner, Cohen, St. Clair, and Gutowski, "Bombshell Filing," 1.

79. Jon Seidel, "Caldero, Acevedo Plead Not Guilty to Federal Charges," *Chicago Sun-Times*, March 6, 2021, 6.

80. Gregory Pratt, "Nearly $95K For Ex-Ald. Solis," *Chicago Tribune*, September 27, 2019, 1.

81. Jon Seidel, "How is Ex-Ald. Solis Still a Free Man?" *Chicago Sun-Times*, August 21, 2020, 1.

82. Author interview with Jesús García, June 21, 2018, Chicago.

83. Author interview with Gilbert Villegas, August 24, 2018, Chicago.

6. Progressives, Socialists, and Machine Politicians

1. Author interview with Aarón Ortíz, August 11, 2018, Chicago.

2. Dan Mihalopoulos, "Political Novice Taking on Rep. Dan Burke," *Chicago Sun-Times*, February 16, 2018, 2.

3. Ortíz interview.

4. Ortíz interview.

5. Ryan Smith, "Meet the Three Young Latino 'Berniecrats,'" *Chicago Reader*, March 29, 2018, 10.

6. Author interview with Jesús García, June 21, 2018, Chicago.

7. Author interview with Aarón Ortíz, August 11, 2018, Chicago.

8. "Our Choices for Illinois House," *Chicago Sun-Times*, February 24, 2020, 16.

9. Carlos Ballesteros, "Lawmakers Push for Bilingual Teachers," *Chicago Sun-Times*, February 4, 2020, 3.

10. Fran Spielman, "Hispanic Oficials Pile on in Flap," *Chicago Sun-Times*, June 19, 2019, 3.

11. Fran Spielman, "Burke Loses Party Post," *Chicago Sun-Times*, March 19, 2020, 3.

12. Lolly Bowean, "25th Ward candidates came to talk housing," *Chicago Tribune*, January 26, 2019, 1.

13. Author interview with Tanya Patiño, March 22, 2019, Chicago.

14. Patiño interview.

15. Patiño interview.

16. Patiño interview.

17. Gregory Pratt, "Rep. Garcia's Endorsements Don't All Pan Out," *Chicago Tribune*, February 28, 2019, 1.

18. Patiño interview.

19. Tina Sfondeles and Matthew Hendrickson, "Burke Easily Extends 50-years Council Reign," *Chicago Sun-Times*, February 27, 2019, 3.

20. Patiño interview.

21. Patiño interview.

22. John Kass, "Boss of New Machine?" *Chicago Tribune*, December 5, 2018, 2.

23. John Kass, "Boss," 2.

24. Author interview with Andre Vasquez, April 19, 2019, Chicago.

25. Vasquez interview.

26. Fran Spielman, "He Could Lose Runoff," *Chicago Sun-Times*, March 24, 2019, 6.

27. Vasquez interview.

28. Vasquez interview.

29. Jon Seidel and Jane Recker, "Newcomer Ousts Longtime 40th Ward Ald. O'Connor," *Chicago Sun-Times*, April 3, 2019, 1.

30. Vasquez interview.

31. Alex V. Hernandez, Mauricio Peña, and Linze Rice, "Democratic Socialists Ready to Work," *Block Club Chicago*, April 3, 2019, 1.

32. Lucie Macias and Leonard Pierce, "Democratic Socialists," *Chicago Tribune*, April 4, 2019, 13.

33. Ryan Smith, "5 Socialists Could Join City Council," *Chicago Sun-Times*, March 3, 2019, 3.

34. Author interview with Joseph Berrios, March 1, 2019, Chicago.

35. Berrios interview.

36. Author interview with Omar Aquino, November 11, 2018, Chicago.

37. "Fire Berrios. Vote for Kaegi," Editorial, *Chicago Tribune*, February 18, 2018, 13.

38. Joseph Berrios interview.

39. Joseph Berrios interview.

40. Sam Charles, "Could Berrios Be Giving Up Ward Post?, *Chicago Sun-Times*, November 27, 2019, 6.

41. Jason Grotto and Hal Dardick, "Berrios' Assessment Practices Flawed," *Chicago Tribune*, February 2018, 1.

42. "Which Preckwinkle Will Lead Democrats?" *Chicago Tribune*, April 19, 2018, 26.

43. Berrios interview.

44. Jeffrey P. Smith, "The Outrageously Important Assessor's Race," *Chicago Tribune*, March 17, 2018, 1.

45. "Fire Berrios. Vote for Kaegi," 13.

46. Charles, "Could Berrios," 6.

47. Berrios interview.

48. Mark Brown, Tim Novak, and Robert Herguth, "What the Feds Want to Know about Joe," *Chicago Sun-Times*, December 18, 2019, 6.

49. Berrios interview.

50. Author interview with Rossana Rodríguez-Sanchez, May 9, 2019, Chicago.

51. Rodríguez-Sanchez interview.

52. Rodríguez-Sanchez interview.

53. Evan Garcia, "33rd Ward Candidate Forum," *Chicago Tonight WTTW. Com/ News*, March 14, 2019.

54. Rodríguez-Sanchez interview.

55. Mark Brown, "Dynasty Slayer Rodriguez Sanchez," *Chicago Sun-Times*, May 1, 2019, 14.

56. "Our final choices for aldermen," *Chicago Tribune*, March 15, 2019, 13.

57. Rodríguez-Sanchez interview.

58. Rodríguez-Sanchez interview.

59. Rodríguez-Sanchez interview.

60. Rodríguez-Sanchez interview.

61. Author interview with Delia Ramirez, September 7, 2018, Chicago.

62. Ramirez interview.

63. Ramirez interview.

64. Ramirez interview.

65. Ramirez interview.

66. "For the Illinois House," *Chicago Tribune*, February 26, 2018, 16.

67. Ramirez interview.

68. Ramirez interview.

69. Ramirez interview.

70. Justin Agrelo, "State Rep. Delia Ramirez," *Chicago Reader*, July 31, 2020, 3.

Epilogue

1. Author interview with Miguel del Valle, March 15, 2019.

2. Bill Ruthhart and John Byrne, "A Shift in City Politics," *Chicago Tribune*, March 7, 2021, 1.

3. Rachel Hinton, Fran Spielman, and Elvia Malagón, "Strength in Numbers Could Boost Latino Political Power," *Chicago Sun-Times*, August 14, 2021.

4. Mary Schmich, "No Longer Lonely on the Bench," *Chicago Tribune*, July 29, 2018, 3.

5. Rick Pearson, "Madigan Picks a 2nd Successor after Forcing Out His First Choice," *Chicago Tribune*, February 6, 2012, 1.

6. Author interview with Celina Villanueva, October 5, 2018, Chicago.

7. "Latinos in the 2016 Election: Illinois." Pew Research Center, January 19, 2016, 1.

8. Author interview with Ramiro Gonzalez, December 1, 2028, Cicero, IL.

9. Nick Villarreal, "Data Points: Illinois Population Loss: Why Immigration is Catching Our Attention," Metropolitan Planning Council, March 22, 2021. https://www.metroplanning.org/news/10061/Data-Points-Illinois-population-loss-why-immigration-is-catching-our-attention.

10. Del Valle interview.

11. Author interview with Jesús García, June 21, 2018.

12. Rick Pearson and Hal Dardick. "Emanuel, allies spent at least $22.8 million to win," *Chicago Tribune*, April 16, 2015, 1.

13. García interview.

14. Author interview with Rossana Rodríguez-Sanchez, May 9, 2019.

Interviews by Author

Anaya, Alma. August 31, 2018. Chicago, IL.
Aquino, Omar. November 11, 2018. Chicago, IL.
Berrios, Joseph. March 1, 2019. Chicago, IL.
Cardona, Felix Jr. August 2, 2019. Chicago, IL.
Del Valle, Miguel. March 15, 2019. Chicago, IL.
García, Jesús. June 21, 2018. Chicago, IL.
Gonzales, Ramiro. November 23, 2018. Cicero, IL.
Joravsky, Ben. February 2, 2019. Chicago, IL.
Lopez, Gabriel. September 14, 2018. Chicago, IL.
Martinez, Virginia. August 31, 2017. Chicago, IL.
Muñoz, Ricardo. June 7, 2018. Chicago, IL.
Ortíz, Aarón. August 11, 2018. Chicago, IL.
Patiño, Tanya. March 22, 2019. Chicago, IL.
Ramirez, Delia. September 7, 2018. Chicago, IL.
Rossana Rodríguez-Sanchez. May 9, 2019. Chicago, IL.
Ruiz, Alicia M. November 30. 2018. Berwyn, IL.
Santiago, Milly. November 5, 2018. Chicago, IL.
Vargas, Blanca M. November 12, 2018. Cicero, IL.
Vasquez, Andre. April 19, 2019. Chicago, IL.
Villanuera, Celina. November 5, 2018. Chicago, IL.
Villegas, Gilbert. August 24, 2018. Chicago, IL.

Works Cited

Amezcua, Mike. "A Machine in the Barrio: Chicago's Conservative Colonia and the Remaking of Latino Politics in the 1960s and 1970s." *Sixties* 12, no. 1 (2019): 95–120.

Amigos for Daley Speech. University of Illinois at Chicago. Richard J. Daley Library, March 26, 1975.

Anderson, Monroe. "The Sawyer Saga: A Journalist, Who Just Happened to be the Mayor's Press Secretary, Speaks." In *The Mayors: The Chicago Political Tradition*, edited by Paul M. Green and Melvin G. Holli, 203–21. Carbondale: Southern Illinois University Press, 2013.

Año Nuevo-Kerr, Louise. "The Chicano Experience in Chicago, 1920–1970." PhD diss., University of Illinois Chicago, 1976.

Badillo, David A. "From *La Lucha* to Latino: Ethnic Change, Political Identity, and Civil Rights in Chicago." In *La Causa: Civil Rights, Social Justice and the Struggle for Equality in the Midwest*, edited by Gilberto Cárdenas, 37–53. Houston: Arte Público Press, 2004.

Belenchia, Joanne. "Latinos and Chicago Politics." In *After Daley: Chicago Politics in Transition*, edited by Samuel K. Gove and Louis H. Masotti, 118–145. Urbana: University of Illinois Press, 1982.

Biles, Roger. *Richard J. Daley: Politics, Race, and the Governing of Chicago*. DeKalb: Northern Illinois University Press, 1995.

Bilyk, Jonathan. "Ex-wife Sues Lawyers." *Cook County Record*, February 9, 2016.

Byrne, Jane. "Declaration of Candidacy of Jane Byrne." Jane Byrne for Mayor. Chicago, April 24, 1978.

———. *My Chicago*. New York: W. W. Norton, 1992.

Chicago Commission on Human Relations. "The Puerto Rican Residents of Chicago," 1966.

Clark, Terry Nichols. "The Irish Ethic and the Spirit of Patronage." *Ethnicity* 2, no. 4 (1975): 305–59.

Cohen, Adam, and Elizabeth Taylor. *American Pharaoh: Mayor Richard J. Daley; His Battle for Chicago and the Nation*. New York: Back Bay Books, 2000.

Córdova, Teresa. "Harold Washington and the Rise of Latino Electoral Politics in Chicago, 1982–1987." In *Chicano Politics and Society in the Late Twentieth Century*, edited by David Montejano, 31–57. Austin: University of Texas Press, 1999.

Cruz, Wilfredo. *City of Dreams: Latino Immigration to Chicago*. Lanham, MD: University Press of America, 2007.

Dominguez, Jaime. "Latinos in Chicago: A Strategy Towards Political Empowerment (1975–2003)." PhD diss., University of Illinois Chicago, 2007.

Erie, Steven P. *Rainbow's End: Irish-Americans and the Dilemmas of Urban Machine Politics, 1840–1985*. Berkeley: University of California Press, 1988.

FitzGerald, Kathleen Whalen. *Brass: Jane Byrne and the Pursuit of Power*. Chicago: Contemporary Books, 1981.

David Fremon. *Chicago Politics Ward by Ward*. Bloomington: Indiana University Press, 1988.

Gradel, Thomas J., and Dick Simpson. *Corrupt Illinois: Patronage, Cronyism, and Criminality*. Urbana: University of Illinois Press, 2015.

Granger, Bill, and Lori Granger. *Fighting Jane*. New York: The Dial Press, 1980.

Green, Paul M. "Mayor Richard J. Daley and the Politics of Good Government." In *The Mayors: The Chicago Political Tradition*, edited by Paul M. Green and Melvin G. Holli, 144–59. Carbondale: Southern Illinois University Press, 2013.

———. "Michael A. Bilandic: The Last of the Machine Regulars." In *The Mayors: The Chicago Political Tradition*, edited by Paul M. Green and Melvin G. Holli, 160–7. Carbondale: Southern Illinois University Press, 2013.

Green, Paul M., and Melvin G. Holli, eds. *The Mayors: The Chicago Political Tradition*. Carbondale: Southern Illinois University Press, 2013.

Grimshaw, William J. *Bitter Fruit: Black Politics and the Chicago Machine, 1931–1991*. Chicago: The University of Chicago Press, 1992.

———. "Harold Washington: The Enigma of the Black Political Tradition." In *The Mayors: The Chicago Political Tradition*, edited by Paul M. Green and Melvin G. Holli, 179–97. Carbondale: Southern Illinois University Press, 2013.

———. "The Daley Legacy: A Declining Politics of Party, Race, and Public Unions." In *After Daley: Chicago Politics in Transition*, edited by Samuel K. Gove and Louis H. Massotti, 57–87. Urbana: University of Illinois Press, 1982.

Gutiérrez, Luis. *Still Dreaming: My Journey from the Barrio to Capitol Hill*. New York: W. W. Norton, 2013.

Hoffman, Abraham. *Unwanted Mexican Americans in the Great Depression: Repatriation Pressures, 1929–1939*. Tucson: The University of Arizona Press, 1974.

Holli, Melvin G. "Jane M. Byrne: To Think the Unthinkable and Do the Undoable." In *The Mayors: The Chicago Political Tradition*, edited by Paul M. Green and Melvin G. Holli, 168–78. Carbondale: Southern Illinois University Press, 2013.

Holli, Melvin G., and Paul M. Green. *Bashing Chicago Traditions: Harold Washington's Last Campaign, Chicago, 1987*. Grand Rapids, MI: William B. Eerdmans, 1989.

Judd, Dennis R., and Annika M. Hinze. *City Politics: The Political Economy of Urban America*. New York: Routledge, 2019.

Kemp, Kathleen A., and Robert L. Lineberry. "The Last of the Great Urban Machines and the Last of the Great Urban Mayors? Chicago Politics, 1955–1977." In *After Daley: Chicago Politics in Transition*, edited by Samuel K. Gove and Louis H. Masotti, 1–27. Urbana: University of Illinois Press, 1982.

Kleppner, Paul. *Chicago Divided: The Making of a Black Mayor*. DeKalb: Northern Illinois University Press, 1985.

Koeneman, Keith. *First Son: The Biography of Richard M. Daley*. Chicago: The University of Chicago Press, 2013.

"Latinos in the 2016 Election: Illinois." Pew Research Center, January 19, 2016.

Maldonado, Edwin. "Contract Labor and the Origins of Puerto Rican Communities in the United States." In *Forging a Community: The Latino Experience in Northwest Indiana, 1919–1975*, edited by James B. Lane and Edward J. Escobar, 201–14. Chicago: Cattail Press, 1987.

Mendoza, Patricia. "Latinos and the Growth of Political Empowerment in Illinois." In *La Causa: Civil Rights, Social Justice and the Struggle for Equality in the Midwest*, edited by Gilberto Cárdenas, 19–35. Houston: Arte Público Press, 2004.

Miller, Alton. *Harold Washington: The Mayor, The Man*. Chicago: Bonus Books, 1989.

"Moreno Sentenced to 11 Years." *U.S. Attorney's Office*, February 19, 2014.

Morton, Richard Allen. *Roger C. Sullivan and the Making of the Chicago Democratic Machine, 1881–1908*. Jefferson, NC: McFarland, 2016.

O'Connor, Len. *Clout: Mayor Daley and His City*. Chicago: Contemporary Books, 1975.

Padilla, Elena. "Puerto Rican Immigrants in New York and Chicago: A Study in Comparative Assimilation." MA Thesis, University of Chicago, 1947.

Police Accountability Task Force. "Restoring Trust Between the Chicago Police and the Communities They Serve." April 2016.

Preston, Michael B. "Black Politics in the Post-Daley Era." In *After Daley: Chicago Politics in Transition*, edited by Samuel K. Gove and Louis H. Masotti, 88–117. Urbana: University of Illinois Press, 1982.

Rakove, Milton L. *We Don't Want Nobody Nobody Sent: An Oral History of the Daley Years*. Bloomington: Indiana University Press, 1979.

Rivlin, Gary. *Fire on the Prairie: Chicago's Harold Washington and the Politics of Race*. New York: Henry Holt, 1992.

Rose, Don. "The Rise of Independent Black Political Power in Chicago." In *The Chicago Freedom Movement: Martin Luther King Jr. and Civil Rights Activism in the North*, edited by Mary Lou Finley, Bernard LaFayette Jr., James R. Ralph Jr., and Pam Smith, 263–268. Lexington: University Press of Kentucky, 2015.

Royko, Mike. *Boss: Richard J. Daley of Chicago*. New York: Plume, 1988.

Rudy Lozano, His Life, His People. A project of the Taller de Estudios Comunitarios. Chicago, 1984.

Salces, Luis M., and Peter W. Colby. "Mañana Will Be Better: Spanish-American Politics in Chicago." In *Latinos and the Political System*, edited by F. Chris Garcia, 195–200. Notre Dame, IN: University of Notre Dame Press, 1988.

San Juan Theater Speech. University of Illinois at Chicago, Richard J. Daley Library, no date.

Santillan, Richard. "Latino Politics in the Midwestern United States: 1915–1986." In *Latinos and the Political System*, edited by F. Chris Garcia, 99–118. Notre Dame, IN: University of Notre Dame Press, 1988.

Spirou, Costas, and Dennis R. Judd. *Building the City of Spectacle: Mayor Richard M. Daley and the Remaking of Chicago*. Ithaca, NY: Cornell University Press, 2016.

Taylor, Paul S. *Mexican Labor in the United States*. Berkeley: University of California Press, 1932.

The Neighborhood Capital Budget Group. "Rebuilding Our Schools." November 9, 1999.

Torres, María de los Angeles. "The Commission on Latino Affairs." In *Harold Washington and the Neighborhoods: Progressive City Government in Chicago, 1983–1987*, edited by Pierre Clavel and Wim Wiewel, 165–187. New Brunswick, NJ: Rutgers University Press, 1991.

Valdez, Virginia. "Chicago Public School's Efforts to Relieve Overcrowding." *Mexican American Legal Defense and Educational Fund*, 2000.

Wilfredo Cruz is associate professor at Columbia College Chicago, where he teaches courses in sociology and political science. He is the author of *City of Dreams: Latino Immigration to Chicago* (Lanham, MD: University Press of America, 2007). Cruz was formerly an assistant press secretary for the late Mayor Harold Washington.